Y0-BUB-462

A Journey with the Saints

A Journey with the Saints

by

THOMAS S. KEPLER

Biography Index Reprint Series

BOOKS FOR LIBRARIES PRESS
FREEPORT, NEW YORK

Reprinted 1971 by arrangement

INTERNATIONAL STANDARD BOOK NUMBER:
0-8369-8070-0

LIBRARY OF CONGRESS CATALOG CARD NUMBER:
70-148223

PRINTED IN THE UNITED STATES OF AMERICA

· TO ·

IRA AND ANITA

JOHN AND OLIVE

BILL AND DOROTHY

Preface

A RELIGIOUS THINKER, surveying the present world situation, said, "The future will not belong to the organizers or the politicians of the traditional type, but to the saints and the prophets. It will be they who will become the creators." A European, viewing the destruction of his native Germany, remarked, "If there is to be a revival in my fatherland, it will happen because here and there will be a saint who lends leadership. For a saint is one who suffers with his fellow-men, yet retains his contact with the power, wisdom, and love of God in a larger degree than is evidenced in ordinary persons."

World leadership today demands persons of "saintly" characteristics. Gerald Heard suggests that a few saints live near our national leaders to lend them advice in times of emergency. Some years ago Rufus Jones asked Baron von Huegel to give the qualities of a saint. In reply he laid down four requisites: (1) a saint is loyal to the faith of the Church; (2) he is heroic; (3) he is recipient of spiritual powers beyond ordinary capacity; (4) he is radiant. Baron von Huegel emphasized "radiance" as the most essential qualification. And it should be, since a "radiant" person is one whose life is "rooted" in God; because of these roots he seems to be a "God-intoxicated" person.

After several years of studying the saints, I am ready to agree with Léon Bloy: "There is only one sorrow, not to be a saint." Although saints come from various cultures and countries, live in different centuries, and face diverse life-situations, they speak a common language—the language of the spirit. They seem to find the spiritual life a festival in which they richly participate in the spiritual banquet which God so freely offers all men. My friendship with the saints reminds me that God's Kingdom can come on earth to the degree that men and women dedicate their talents to the ways of the saints.

The life of a saintly person is conditioned in the following ways:

1. His life is imbued with a deep love of the Christian religion as a way of "feeling at home" in the universe.

2. He lives with a radiance because his spirit is rooted in God's Spirit. "A saint is a person who has quit worrying about himself" because his life is centered in God. With Jacob Böehme he says, "Though my head and my hand be at labor, yet doth my heart dwell in God."

3. He starts each day with these words: "May the image of Christ radiate through me this day in each life-situation."

4. He asks that God use him as an instrument of His love to bear the burdens of his fellow-men. Like Saint Francis, the saint loves "not humanity but men."

5. He believes that before God's Kingdom can arrive in society, it must first begin in him.

6. He has humility, caused by his belief that life is too much trouble unless he can live for something that

is big. And most of all, his life is lost in the Bigness of God.

7. He feels that every person—regardless of color, race, creed or nation—is a person in whom lie the possibilities of becoming a saint. With Robert Southwell he says, "Not where I breathe but where I love, I live."

8. He desires to use the results of prayer and devotion to better the world.

9. He believes that the two great secrets for becoming a saint lie in "the imitation of Christ" and "the practice of the presence of God."

10. His daily preparation for sainthood is in these words:

By all means use sometimes to be alone.
Salute thyself; see what thy soul doth wear.
Dare to look into thy chest; for 'tis thy own.

The saints feel that social change in the world must first begin with individuals. Saints are not geniuses, but normal persons whose powers have become greatly magnified by God. Sometimes this revolution within persons is sudden and dynamic. Catherine of Genoa, of the famous Guelph family from which two popes came, married a wealthy husband in 1463. For ten years they squandered their wealth and ministered to their worldly desires for luxury. Then came a sudden hatred of worldly dissipation. They gave their wealth to the Franciscans; they contributed their home for use as a hospital except for two rooms in which they lived; the remaining days of their lives they ministered to the patients in this hospital.

Sometimes the inner revolution is gradual. Austin Phelps, who taught in Andover Theological Seminary until shortly before his death in 1890, kept a spiritual diary. On the eve of his ordination to the Congregational Church, he wrote in his diary: "I promised God tonight that I would do anything if he would only give me a chance to serve Him. I would work hard, I would stay poor, I would make any sacrifice if he would only guide me and help me, give me opportunity, and finally success in my efforts for Him." On the last page of his diary were these words, written with trembling fingers a few days before his death: "Led by His Spirit all the way."

The secret of the revolution in the lives of the saints lies in the fact that their lives are centered in God. They never seem hurried, they have a large leisure, they trouble little about their influence; they refer the smallest things to God —they live in God. When the revolution in their lives occurs, they seldom leave the church but attempt instead to reform the weaknesses within the church. They rededicate themselves to the betterment of institutions of which they are members. Revolutions without saints usually result in ruthless tyranny and bestial living: this is evidenced in recent revolutions begun by Hitler, Stalin and Mussolini. In our present world, the call is for a spiritual revolution in which Christian saints become leaders.

The saints always seem to have an unassuming heroism, so that they can turn apparent defeat into victory. The Duke of Wellington, in comparing the French and the British soldiers, said, "The British soldiers are not braver than the French soldiers. They are merely braver *five minutes longer.*" The saints are like that. Wherein the ordinary man loses heart, the saint will be braver "five minutes longer." Francis of Assisi wished to become an Umbrian hermit so that he could experience a quiet life of prayer. He was forced instead to move into preaching, yet he was able to turn an apparent disappointment into a victory which began the Franciscan order of monks. His life, like the lives of other saints, was an "imitation of Christ" and a "practice of the presence of God." Thomas Aquinas once said to Bonaventura, "Show me your library." Bonaventura took Thomas Aquinas to his cell and pointed to a crucifix before which he prayed. "There it is," he said. The courage of the saints issues from the heroism of One who was dauntless until the end.

The saints are known by acts of redemptive love among their fellow-men. Frank Laubach teaching people to read and write in Mindanao, Kagawa helping the poor in the slums in Japan, Schweitzer taking medical aid to Africa, John Woolman denouncing slavery in New Jersey, William Law in England giving milk to his poor neighbors, are illustrative of redemptive deeds of the saints. Muriel Lester, a modern saint born of English nobility, ministers to the needs of the poor at Kingsley Hall in London. One of her books bears this dedication: "Dedicated to the common people by whose sweat our grain is produced, our livestock tended, our houses built, our clothes made, our furnaces stoked, our factories manned, and who keep the world sane." Her dedication is symbolic of all saints who keep alive their concern for the needs of mankind.

We are "called to be saints." The wisdom of the forty saints from various centuries is ours to contemplate within these pages. The way that we use their insights in the present will help determine the kind of civilization in which we are to live. May this journey with the saints lead its readers to some new vistas of spiritual living!

The forty studies in these pages first circulated in the columns of daily metropolitan newspapers. Many people shared the thoughts of the persons within this book. This book is the result of the widespread request that these daily articles be brought together into a single volume. The author naturally hopes that those who cultivate the friendship of these saintly persons will find an enduring spiritual fellowship. The saints are wonderful personalities to number among your friends!

THOMAS S. KEPLER

Oberlin, Ohio
May 10, 1951

Contents

A Journey with the Saints

Cyprian 200?-258

THE SCENE is a garden in Carthage, North Africa. It is the middle of the third century of the Christian era and a middle-aged man, Cyprian by name, is writing to his friend Donatus. This is what he says: "This seems a cheerful world, Donatus, when I view it from this fair garden under the shadow of these vines. But if I climbed some great mountain and looked out over the wide lands you know very well what I would see. Brigands on the high roads, pirates on the seas, in the amphitheatres men murdered to please applauding crowds, under all roofs misery and selfishness. It is really a bad world, Donatus, an incredibly bad world. Yet in the midst of it I have found a quiet and holy people. They have discovered a joy which is a thousand times better than any pleasure of this sinful life. They are despised and persecuted but they care not. They have overcome the world. These people, Donatus, are the Christians—and I am one of them."

Seventeen centuries have passed since Cyprian wrote those words. The problems of living have become more complex, for a machine age and a global war seem to make "brigands on the high roads" and "pirates on the seas" rather small evils; yet the Christian today believes that he has a way to meet twentieth-century problems as vitally as did Cyprian in the third century. Christianity has not become outmoded; as a way of living it has remained vital and fresh. Jesus' insights, when properly interpreted, have shown the Christian "the way, and the truth, and the life" for every century.

No man ever loved the church more deeply than Cyprian.

Born into a wealthy Carthaginian family, and well-educated, he became a Christian in 246. By 249 he was made bishop of Carthage. His church leadership was during the persecutions of the Roman emperors, Decius and Valerian; under Valerian Cyprian was beheaded in 258. Cyprian was forced to direct the church for several years from exile. For his flight into exile he was criticized as being a coward, yet he meant it for the good of the church. His circumstance was similar to that of church leaders in Germany during the recent Nazi persecutions: to stay in Germany meant death, while to flee temporarily to another country in exile meant a continuing leadership. Men like Cyprian, who remained faithful to the church during Hitler's tyrannical rule, saved the church in Germany.

Albert Einstein, brilliant Jewish scientist, who had little interest in the church before World War II, expected university teachers and editors in Germany to stand for freedom when the revolution in Germany began; but they were silenced in a few weeks. Only the church leaders had the courage and persistence to stand for intellectual truth and moral freedom. Such loyalty to church ideals in time of persecution won Einstein's praise. Cyprian, in similar fashion, was a courageous leader in the time of Decius, for he deeply loved the church. Hear his words: "There is no salvation outside of the church . . . He can no longer have God for his father, who has not the church for his mother . . . Whoever he may be and whatever he may be, he who is not in the church of Christ is not a Christian."

Cyprian would be critical of many of us today who are church members. A recent survey shows that one fourth of the church members in the United States take an active interest in the affairs of the church, or attend its services of worship. In the eyes of many, there seems to be little moral and spiritual difference between church and non-church people. The first-century Christians won converts to their cause because they outlived, outthought and outdied pagans. One of the ways we today can fight communism in the world is by living our Christianity courageously and sincerely. As Cyprian, also, saw the church as the institution to unify the world, so we today can be loyal to the church universal. The organization of the World Church Council in Amsterdam, Holland, in 1949 is a step in the right direction. Through the World Church we could make these words come alive:*

We men of earth have here the stuff
Of Paradise—we have enough!
We need no other stones to build
The Temple of the Unfulfilled;
No other ivory for the doors—
No other marble for the floors—
No other cedar for the beam
And dome of man's immortal dream.

Here on the paths of every-day—
Here on our common human way
Is all the busy gods would take
To build a Heaven, to mold and make
New Edens. Ours the stuff sublime
To build Eternity in time!

* Edwin Markham, "Earth Is Enough" from *Shoes of Happiness and Other Poems.* Copyright 1915, 1932 by Doubleday, Page and Company. Reprinted by permission of Virgil Markham.

Augustine 354-430

I VIVIDLY remember an April afternoon in my sixth-floor apartment in Cambridge, Massachusetts, about twenty-five years ago. I was reading *The Confessions of Saint Augustine.* Here is a man, I thought, who would have understood the struggles which all of us are facing, the temptation to do wrong and the urge to do right. The centuries may place a halo around him, but in his own day his feet were on the ground. He arrived at his sainthood through a long spiritual struggle.

Augustine was born in Tagaste,* North Africa, of a pagan father, Patricius (later to become a Christian), and a devout Christian mother, Monica. In the early days of his education his curiosity was aroused when he could find no reference to Jesus Christ in Cicero's *Hortensius.* While a student of twenty years of age he became the father of a child born out of wedlock. Brilliant, willful, studious, skeptical, sometimes licentious, the story of Augustine is the story of human nature. At thirty, still fighting the battle of flesh and spirit, he prayed: "Give me chastity, but not yet!"

Tremendous influences were to bring about the conversion of Augustine to Christianity. One of these was Bishop Ambrose of Milan, whose sermons and counsel pierced the conscience of Augustine. Sometimes we hear about "the foolishness of preaching," and some preaching perhaps has little relationship to life problems. But Bishop Ambrose con-

* Now called Souk-Ahras.

vinced Augustine. Perhaps Bishop Ambrose, who felt the urgency of preaching, could say:

I preached as never sure to preach again,
And as a dying man to dying men.

In 387 he baptized Augustine into the Christian faith.

The year preceding his baptism, Augustine discusses the troubles of his soul with a pupil Alypius. Augustine is torn with inner conflict. He breaks into tears and throws himself to the ground, sobbing, "How long! tomorrow and tomorrow!" In a nearby garden he hears a child singing, "Tolle lege, tolle lege!" (take up and read, take up and read). These words of a childish game he applies to himself. Calmly he returns to his house, picks up a volume of Paul's letters and reads from the Epistle to the Romans, "Not in rioting and drunkenness, not in chambering and wantonness, not in strife and envying; but put ye on the Lord Jesus Christ, and make not provision for the flesh in the lusts thereof." Showing the passage to Alypius, they notice the words which follow, "Him that is weak in the faith receive ye." These words they apply to themselves.

In 391, at the urgent requests of multitudes, Augustine was ordained a priest in the Catholic Church at Hippo. Here he remained until his death in 430, four years as a priest, the rest of his years as a bishop. Because of Augustine this small seaport became famous through the Christian centuries. Here he wrote his *Confessions* and *City of God.* Here he grew into one of the great Christian theologians, one who wrote many doctrines for the Church.

Augustine was deeply aware of the immensity of God's grace working in the life of man. There seemed to him so little that we can do to repay God for His grace given to us;

yet we can do so in our simple acts each day. In explanation of Psalm 34 Augustine commented to his friends at Hippo: "If you are singing a hymn you are praising God . . . Then the hymn comes to an end and it is time for a meal; if you keep yourself from overeating, you will be praising God. Are you a rural laborer? Then be sure there are no weeds left in the ground you are digging, and once again this will be an occasion of praising God. Thus by the innocency of your works you will be praising God all the day long."

Augustine's yearning for salvation through close companionship with God is the quest of the ages: "O! that I might repose on Thee! O, that Thou wouldst enter into my heart, and inebriate it, that I may forget my ills, and embrace Thee, my sole good . . . Thou madest us for Thyself and our heart is restless, until it repose in Thee."

Reared in the paganism of the Roman Empire, Augustine saw the coming decay of that society (which occurred in 486). In its place he envisioned "The City of God," the body of Christian believers who compose the Church. What might our civilization in the year 1951 become if 650,000,000 members of "The City of God," the Church, became centered in God, conscious in daily acts of God's grace, and loyal to the universal Church! How fresh Augustine's suggestions are for the twentieth century!

Benedict of Nursia 480?-?543

NEAR DUBUQUE, Iowa, among the hills along the Mississippi River is a Trappist monastery where sixty-four monks reside. Sixty-one of them have taken the vow of silence. Were you to be there at two o'clock some morning you would see these monks quietly file into a chapel for mass; before the day had ended they would have spent eight hours attending mass. When they work in the fields during the day, they say nothing verbally to each other. Through this monastic kind of living they hope to achieve not only salvation for themselves, but also to store up salvation for their fellowmen. This order originated in the Abbey of La Trappe in the seventeenth century, when the Cistercian monastic order had degenerated.

The monastic movement arose and developed with men like Jerome, Bernard of Clairvaux and Benedict, who felt the difficulty of "being Christian in an un-Christian society," especially after Constantine gave sanction to the church at the beginning of the fourth century. As the church began to reform the Roman Empire with Christianity, the pagan values of the Empire began to filter back into the church. Hence the monasteries developed as places where Christian values could be lived without the influence of the pagan values of the world. Many Christians sought the monasteries as places for "saving themselves from the world." But after a time monasteries began to degenerate. Benedict of Nursia arose as the great reformer of monastic life.

Born of a good family in the Umbrian village of Nursia and educated at Rome, Benedict grew disgusted with the evils of the city and sought the life of a hermit in a cave of the mountains at Subiaco, forty miles from Rome. Here for three years he lived a life of prayer and discipline, his place of refuge known only to a monk, Romulus. Reports of his piety spread, and he became head of a monastic group. About 529 he founded a new monastery on the hill of Monte Cassino, halfway between Rome and Naples, and remained there until his death. This place became the ideal pattern for monastic life, with its regulation laid down in the "Rule" composed by Benedict soon after its establishment.

As compared with some monastic orders, Benedict's rules seem fairly lenient. Benedict viewed a monastery as a permanent, self-supporting garrison of Christ's soldiers, where absolute obedience, simplicity of living and constant occupation prevail. His monks had sufficient sleep (about eight hours a night), good food, proper clothes. The monks arose between 1:30 and 3:00 A.M.; they refrained from flesh meat, and fasted until noon or 3:00 P.M. each day. Four or five hours a day were spent in religious exercises; six hours were given to work; four hours were devoted to reading. In the prologue to the *Rule* Benedict says: "As we advance in the religious life and faith, we shall run the way of God's commandments with expanded hearts and unspeakable sweetness of love; so that never departing from His guidance and persevering in the monastery in His doctrine until death, we may by patience share in the sufferings of Christ, and be found worthy to be coheirs with Him of His kingdom."

While most of us are unable to flee to a Trappist or a Benedictine monastery, we are nevertheless convinced that we must have a "rule" for our living in the world. Without discipline, our days and years count for little. Of all designs given for the modern day, Richard C. Cabot in 1914 laid down one of the best in his book, *What Men Live By*. In this volume, which went through thirty-three printings in the first decade of its publication, Dr. Cabot gives a fourfold rule: to work, play, love and worship.

The way we are able to balance discipline of work, play, love and worship will determine the joy and purpose of our lives. At the center of these four disciplines, worship is tremendously important. In worship man tries to determine how best he can ally work, play and love; he also places himself in such a position that God's energy, wisdom and love can supplement his human frailty. In worship the thoughtful person, concerned with a disciplined life, asks with a French poet,

What! you haven't any star—and you're going on the sea?
You're going into battle with no music?
You're going on a trip without a book?
What! you have no love and yet you talk of living?

As Benedict's rule played an important role in giving a proper balance to life in the monastery, so Dr. Cabot's "rule" of work, play, love and worship will prove a worthy guide for us who live the disciplined life in the world.

Bernard of Clairvaux 1091-1153

On a high hill northwest of Dijon, France, sat a feudal castle, Fontaines-les-Dijon. Here in 1091 Bernard was born to parents of Burgundian nobility.

One evening, when Bernard was sixteen, during a dinner his mother Aleph had given for a company of priests, she fell ill and died as the priests intoned a litany for her. Aleph had planned for the life of the cloister but had married instead. She hoped that one of her seven children might realize the monastic life she failed to achieve, and she disciplined them in prayer and renunciation of worldly pleasures. She resided with Bernard at Chatillon where he went for his schooling. Bernard had been his mother's ideal, and his attachment to her was deeply disrupted at her death. For years he recited daily penitential psalms for her; he had visions of her. One of these visions when he was twenty-two caused his self-dedication to religion.

In the third century of the Christian era the cry of Christians was, "Outside of the church there is no salvation." After Emperor Constantine in 325 asked his subjects to embrace Christianity, the church began to be influenced by the paganism of the world. It became difficult for people to be Christians in such an un-Christian society. Monasteries thus became refuges for those who wanted to live the Christian life seriously and to avoid worldly temptations. Some of the monasteries fell into disrepute, as they grew wealthy and spiritual discipline grew lax.

Bernard at twenty-two joined a monastery at Citeaux, ruled by Stephen. Five of his brothers and many others soon joined his monastery. Bernard was active in their training. At twenty-five Stephen sent Bernard from Citeaux with twelve men to start a monastery at Clairvaux. Bernard was so successful in his leadership that sixty-eight branches of Clairvaux were founded. The Cistercian order of which Bernard and Stephen were members expanded during Bernard's life to almost five hundred monasteries.

The secret of Bernard's success was two-fold. First, he set up rigid requirements for monastic living. As a great athlete trains for his games, so the spiritual athlete trains for his Christian tasks. Barley bread and beech-leaf salad composed the diet for Bernard's monks; hard labor with ax, rake and sickle was their daily routine as they cleared the wilderness; spiritual meditation and the round of masses each day were required. In these austerities Bernard found great joy. He rejoiced in the feast of God's Spirit, as he fasted of worldly pleasures. He would rather pray than sleep. His monks shared his enthusiasm. Second, Bernard was a practical man. Arable land, drained swamps, wool trade, breeding of cattle, sheep and poultry, resulted from Bernard's monastic organization. Bernard's labors brought a renewal to the monastic life.

At the heart of Bernard's thinking and living was the "imitation of Christ" through humility and love. He stressed the humanity of Christ at a time when speculative theologians were "losing" Jesus in their abstract arguments. Regarding the need of Christlike humility Bernard wrote: "It is not enough to be subject to God unless you are also subject to every human creature for God's sake; whether to the abbot as ruler or the priors appointed to him. I say more: Be subject to your equals and even to your inferiors. For thus it becomes us to fulfill all righteousness. If you wish to be perfect, make advances to him that is less than you; defer to your inferior, bow to your junior . . . Humility is the mother of salvation." This humility was tied to unselfish love in the imitation of Christ.

Booker T. Washington has set a dramatic example of the humility and love about which Bernard speaks. One day when he arrived at a town for an address, the white cab driver refused to drive him to the auditorium. Mr. Washington said to the driver, "All right, then. You get in the rider's seat, and I'll drive you to the auditorium!" Perhaps many of us need this humility and love as we try to relieve the misery of the world.

"From Him do the saints derive the odor of sanctity; from Him also do they shine as lights," said Bernard about Christ. While most of us are not able to imitate Christ in a monastery apart from the world, we can practice Bernard's suggestions *in* the world where we try to imitate Christ. Bernard is, in the words of a child who remembered saints painted on cathedral windows, "a man the light shines through." Through Bernard shone the light of one who was the Light of the World! How much the world needs men like Bernard instead of Hitlers, Mussolinis and Stalins!

Jan van Ruysbroeck 1293-1381

TWO STUDENTS from Paris once visited Jan van Ruysbroeck for the purpose of being taught spiritual truths. After their conversation with Ruysbroeck, they left dissatisfied, for he had said to them, "You will be as holy as you wish to be." His words are true in all areas of life; we are as expert as we want to be.

A young man wanted to be a great writer; so he disciplined himself to write 5,000 words a morning. He received many rejection slips from editors, for his writings were not good. Finally his contributions began to be published. The young man who wished to be a great writer was Bernard Shaw. Another young man wished to be a great artist. Today his murals hang in the capitals of Europe, in Buckingham Palace, in the Houses of Parliament. His name is Frank O. Salisbury, and here is what he said of himself: "There were others in my class of greater talent, but they refused the discipline of hard work." "You will be as holy as you want to be" serves as a guide for those who desire to be artists in spiritual living, as the wish to be great is inherent in the fields of writing, art, science or business. The "wish to be" is the first requisite for those who will achieve.

A friend once said to me, "One of my lowest moments, as I now look back, was a New Year's eve when I felt no urge within myself to improve." He was as "holy" as he wanted to be—which is a sign of danger in religious living.

Jan van Ruysbroeck is one of the great Flemish saints. Born near Brussels, Belgium, he lived in the outdoors, in the forests, among the birds and animals. At eleven years of age, when many boys "ran away to sea," he ran away from home to consecrate himself to God. At twenty-four he was ordained a priest. For twenty-five years he ministered to a busy parish of Brussels. Yet he learned the secret of living a quiet life amid the noise and hostilities of the city. He knew the secret of "The Labour and Rest of Love": "In one single moment and at the same time," he says, "love labors and rests in its beloved. And the one is strengthened by the other; for the loftier the love, the greater is the rest, and the greater is the rest, the closer is the love; for the one lives in the other, and he who loves not rests not, neither does he who rests not know aught of love." Hatred, jealousy, suspicion and fear sap our energy and our inner serenity: love, forgiveness and sympathy invite energy into our spirits.

In our modern language, we speak about religion integrating, or holding together, a person. Ruysbroeck was aware of this: "Unity is this," he wrote, "that a man feel himself to be gathered together with all his powers in the unity of his heart. Unity brings inward peace and restfulness of heart. Unity is a bond which draws together body and soul, heart and senses, and all outward and inward powers and encloses them in the union of love." We speak about religion bringing help to a person in time of stress. As a person trains his body for an athletic contest, so he trains his spirit to run the race of life. As a person becomes interested in good books, music, friends, beliefs, worship, moral acts, he discovers that his loyalty to these high values breeds inner strength. One morning Toscanini was rehearsing a Beethoven symphony with his orchestra. When the symphony ended, the men in the orchestra arose and applauded Toscanini.

When their applause stopped, he said, "Men, don't applaud me. It's not I; it's Beethoven." But the secret of Toscanini's success was not only that he had mastered Beethoven, but that Beethoven had also mastered him. Similarly, as we master fine moral and spiritual values, they in turn master us. That is how religion brings help in time of difficulty. Religion thus brings unity or integration of man, he "feels himself to be gathered together with all his powers in the unity of his heart."

At fifty years of age, Jan van Ruysbroeck sought the life of a hermit in the forest of Soignies near Brussels; here he lived until his death thirty-eight years later. During these years, he built a monastery, wrote at least eleven books, taught and administered the monastery. He was an active member of the Friends of God who emphasized the spiritual growth of a Christian toward perfection. He saw God as the sea which ebbs and flows in each life: "This flowing forth of God always demands a flowing back; for God is the Sea that ebbs and flows, pouring without ceasing into all His beloved, according to the need and merits of each."

In 1908 Jan van Ruysbroeck was officially beatified as "Blessed John." And such he was, for he saw the relation of man and God as akin to a spiritual marriage. The boy who "ran away to God" was to become one of the great spiritual leaders of the Christian centuries.

Rulman Merswin 1307-1382

"He was 'dying' at fifty-three—but he lived to ninety-eight!" John D. Rockefeller is thus described by a biographer, who ascribes his prolonged years to the dedication of himself and his money to philanthropic causes like the University of Chicago, Tuskegee Institute for Negroes, the Rockefeller Foundation. In the fourteenth century lived another philanthropist, Rulman Merswin of Strasbourg, who found his life purpose in giving to others. In 1367 Merswin came to his dramatic conversion. He was a wealthy banker, a man of power, but he felt that he had missed the goal of living. A plague of Black Death in the Rhine Valley caused him to think deeply about his own life and death. After seeking the counsel of John Tauler, Strasbourg's greatest preacher, he made his about-face. Near Strasbourg beyond the mills and tanneries on the Ill River was Green Isle, where a church and convent had been built a hundred years earlier. Merswin sold his bank, bought Green Isle as a place for religious retreats, and with his wife dedicated himself and his wealth to God. He lived his last twelve years there.

The world was out of joint in the fourteenth century; something had gone wrong and Merswin gave himself to its betterment. When he first gave up his wealth, he felt it a way to atone for his sins. After ten weeks of simplified living, as he was meditating in a garden on the evils of mankind, he felt a keen hatred of the world; he spent a year in ascetic practices, which almost caused his death. It was then that he saw a higher type of salvation, the living of a disciplined spiritual life *in* the world.

Merswin remained a loyal churchman. He was faithful to the sacraments, holy days, holy places, the pope as the head of the church. Yet he knew that something was wrong with organized religion, and he put little hope in church leaders to lead people out of worldly corruption. He felt that among "the friends of God," the laymen of his time, lay the betterment of the world.

The contemporary relation of the church to the needs of the world is similar to that of Merswin's time. *Fortune* magazine not many months ago pointed out that too often the church has little to offer as a solution to the world's misery; sometimes this is true. The church will help the world only as its "friends of God," or laymen, are consecrated with their wealth and ability. In the United States, 5 per cent of the people were church members in 1783, 15 per cent in 1835, while today 56 per cent belong to the church. Yet a recent survey of 7,600 American homes showed 2,900 without a Bible; in our country a major crime is performed each 22 seconds; in a recent year, half a million dollars was spent by twelve leading peace groups, while five billion dollars was spent in gambling and four billion dollars on liquor. We can despair about the misery in the world, but like Rulman Merswin we can dedicate our talents to its remedy.

We need a bifocal vision as we see the misery about us. We need to focus our view on world problems, where we talk of world peace, world fellowship, world brotherhood. But we also need our closer focus on the problems in our homes, offices, factories, neighborhoods. During World War II, a cablegram was sent to Hitler by a state conference of ministers, in which they protested his treatment of the Jews in Germany. One of the ministers in reporting the cablegram said that while he was thoroughly in sympathy with the cablegram sent to Hitler, he did feel that some ministers and their church members were perhaps a bit more concerned about Hitler's treatment of the Jews in Germany than they were with their aid to the underprivileged in their own state. World problems related to race relations, war and peace, industry and education, are initially solved in the neighborhoods where we live. The Christian is his brother's keeper.

Green Isle was a setting where men could live God's will in a small communal way. It was to be a cheerful place, where temperance in all ways of living was practiced. Said Merswin: "Whoever among you is not thankful has not the love of God in him; he should come to live with me and my comrades, who find themselves as one heart in our love to God, and we accept all trials with untroubled hearts." But he saw salvation as not just for those on Green Isle. After his conversion he longed to go joyfully among the heathen to tell them of the Christian faith. He believed that the gospel of Christ was powerful enough to save mankind. In his own language he could say:

This is our faith tremendous,
Our wild hope, who shall scorn,
That in the name of Jesus
*The world shall be reborn!**

But world salvation began with people like himself, who would dedicate their wealth and their talent to God's work for the world.

* Vachel Lindsay, "Foreign Missions in Battle Array" from *Collected Poems*. Copyright 1925 by The Macmillan Company. Reprinted by permission of the publishers.

Gerhard Groot 1340-1384

"FIFTEEN YEARS ago I was teaching religion on an American college campus," said a friend to me. "I found myself in a state of religious perplexity. I seemed to be unhappy as I found my religious ideas shifting. At that time I began to read *The Imitation of Christ* each morning before I taught my classes. That book of devotional readings 'saved' me into a new enthusiasm for daily living. It brought me inner strength. It helped me to get along with myself."

My friend was one of many thousands who have found *The Imitation of Christ* helpful. John Wesley said about it, "A person will never be satisfied with it, though it were read a thousand times over." A Roman Catholic scholar remarked, "After the Gospel the *Imitation* undoubtedly is the book that reflects with the greatest perfection the light of Jesus Christ brought down from heaven." I remember seeing the place in Brussels, Belgium, where Edith Cavell was shot by a firing squad in World War I, and seeing her words, "Patriotism is not enough." Back of the courage of Edith Cavell was a much-read and well-marked copy of *The Imitation of Christ.* The popularity of this religious classic has gone through more than three thousand editions.

Gerhard Groot is the author of *The Imitation of Christ.* He was a wealthy lawyer of Deventer, Holland, educated at universities in Deventer, Aachen, Prague, Paris and Cologne. At twenty-six he was sent on a mission to the Pope at Avignon. At thirty-four, after an illness, he gave his Deventer mansion, excepting two rooms, to the Sisters of the Common Life, and became a Carthusian monk. From

1379 to 1383 he was Holland's greatest lay preacher. In his preaching he criticized some of the weaknesses of the church, and stressed the authority for individual religion within a person. His preaching license was revoked by the Bishop of Utrecht. He then retired to his estate at Deventer, where he wrote *The Imitation of Christ.* After a year in retirement he died, after ministering to a friend who was ill of the plague. Fifty-seven years after Groot's death, the *Imitation* was edited by Thomas a Kempis at Mt. Agnes near Zwolle.

"My worst enemy is myself," said a woman to me recently. "I want to get along with myself, but I don't know how." I suggested that she read *The Imitation of Christ,* since its main theme is "Conquer yourself where you are." Too many of us are too busy doing too many things. An Australian said of us, "You Americans are more concerned with the fruits than with the roots of living." For this hurry in our living, Gerhard Groot advises the use of solitude and silence: "Seek a convenient time to retire into yourself, and meditate on God's kind deeds . . . If you will withdraw yourself from useless talk and idle goings-about, as well as from novelties and gossips, you will find leisure enough and suitable for good meditation." The chief beatitude from the *Imitation* is "Blessed are those who are glad to have time to spare for God."

The happiness of many people is spoiled because they are more concerned with moving to a new position than in enjoying the work where they are. Gerhard Groot saw danger to the person who is always keeping his eye on a better position. "The imagination and the desire for change of residence have deceived many a one," he wrote. "They who wander much abroad seldom thereby become holy . . .

Thou mayest change thy position but not better thyself." He felt that to change positions was often merely the shifting of one set of problems for a new set. As I look about in my generation I see great men staying in one position the entirety of their careers: Rufus Jones, the Quaker philosopher, taught only at Haverford College; Ralph W. Sockman, nationally known radio preacher, has been at Christ's Church in New York since his seminary days; William Allen White spent his life as a newspaper editor in Emporia, Kansas; Arthur Hewitt, famous rural preacher, has remained all his life within walking distance of his birthplace in Vermont. All of these men have achieved national and world greatness because they conquered themselves where they were.

When Groot was forced into retirement by the Bishop of Utrecht, he learned to have confidence in God while his opponents were saying evil things about him. His words of consolation, when people are criticizing us, are sound: "If thou art guilty, think how thou wouldst gladly amend thyself . . . If thou art conscious of nothing wrong on thy part, consider that thou wouldst gladly suffer this for God's sake . . . When thou shrinkest from being abased and disgraced for thy faults, it is evident that thou art not yet truly humble, nor truly dead to the world, and the world is not crucified to thee . . . Harken to my words, and thou shalt not care for ten thousand words spoken by men."

Both Groot and Edward Everett Hale saw personal criticisms in proper perspective. A parishioner of Dr. Hale noticed a small non-complimentary item about himself in a Boston paper. In a ruffled state of mind, he asked Dr. Hale what to do about the article. Dr. Hale replied, "One half who bought the paper did not notice the article. One half who saw it did not read it. One half who read it did not remember it. One half who remembered it thought it untrue. The half who thought it true don't count. I'd do nothing about it!"

It is easy to understand why *The Imitation of Christ* is the most widely read devotional writing excepting the Bible. In Francis of Assisi's words, *The Imitation* invites us: "Come, now, let us begin to be Christians."

Thomas More 1478-1535

IN JUNE, 1535, Sir Thomas More is a prisoner in the London Tower for criticizing the marriage of King Henry VIII to Anne Boleyn, and for not recognizing the King of England as the temporal head of the church. Several weeks before his execution on July 7, 1535, he writes a meditation:

Give me thy grace, good Lord,
To set the world at nought,
To set my mind fast on thee.
And not to hang upon the blast of men's mouths.
To be content to be solitary,
Not to long for world company,
Little and little utterly to cast off the world,
And rid my mind of all the business thereof.
Gladly to be thinking of God,
Piteously to call for his help,
To lean upon the comfort of God,
Busily to labor to love him.

Several days before his death, he wrote a prayer which contains these words: "Good Lord, give me the grace, in all my fear and agony to have recourse to that great fear and wonderful agony that thou, my sweet Savior, hadst at the Mount of Olives before the most bitter passion, and in the meditation thereof, to conceive ghostly comfort and consolation profitable to my soul. Almighty God, take from me all vainglorious minds, all appetites of mine own praise, all envy, covetise, gluttony, sloth, and lechery, all wrathful affections, all appetite of revenging, all desire or delight of other folks' harm, all pleasure in provoking any person to wrath and anger, all delight of exprobation or insulation against any person in their affliction and calamity. And give me, good Lord, an humble, lowly, quiet, peaceable, patient, charitable, kind, tender, and pitiful mind, with all my works, and all my words, and all my thoughts, to have a taste of thy Holy, Blessed Spirit."

The man behind these courageous and tender words, made Chancellor to King Henry VIII in 1529, was the first layman ever to hold that coveted office. By the time he was thirty, More's professional income was 400 pounds a year (equivalent to about $100,000 today). He owned a beautiful estate at Chelsea. Each Friday Thomas More retired from his heavy duties as Lord High Chancellor and King's Counselor to a little building on the Chelsea estate for spiritual reading and prayer. In these meditations More found a resource which kept him courageous through the Tower imprisonment and the facing of execution.

In our times of hurry and tension we can learn much about the "eloquence of silence" from Thomas More. Admiral Byrd thrilled many with his excursion to the South Pole a few years ago, where he was "alone." While apart from his companions with only radio connections, and then with the radio communication broken, Admiral Bryd found a new perspective of life. Here is what he wrote: "I did take away something that I had not fully possessed before: appreciation of the sheer beauty and miracle of being alive, and a humble set of values . . . I live more simply now, and with more peace . . . There were moments when I felt more *alive* than at any other time in my life."* Middleton Murry, after World War I, was disillusioned and contem-

* Richard E. Byrd, *Alone*. Copyright 1938 by G. P. Putnam's Sons.

plated suicide. After the death of his wife Katherine Mansfield, he sought silence and solitude. Here is what he found: "A moment came when the darkness of that ocean changed to light, the cold to warmth: when it swept in one great wave over the shores and the frontier of myself, when it bathed me and I was renewed; when the room was filled with a Presence, and I knew that I was not alone, that I never could be alone any more; that the universe held no menace, for I was a part of it; that in some way for which I had sought in vain so many years, I belonged; and because I belonged I was no longer I, but something different, which could never be afraid in the old ways or cowardly with the old cowardice."*

An American humorist suggests that we throw away our speedometers and buy alarm clocks! We need to be awakened to some new purpose of life instead of seeing how fast we can live. In a country which manufactures over four million pounds of aspirin a year, we need experiences which can save us from our headaches and give us poise. The alternation from days of busy activity to a day of meditation at Chelsea each Friday deepened and strengthened the spirit of Thomas More. A balance of work and meditation can aid us too. We should remember the parable of the iceberg, unaffected and standing straight amid the turbulence of northern waters, because six-sevenths of the iceberg lies below the surface of the water. Depth and poise are partners in Christian experience.

Out of his meditation, Sir Thomas More in 1516 conceived *Utopia*. Though it was a satirical writing, it contained many basic truths. In it he tells of the conversation which he and Peter Giles have with Ralph Hythlodaye who

* J. Middleton Murry, *God*. Copyright 1929 by Harper & Brothers.

sailed with Amerigo Vespucci. As Hythlodaye visits England, he compares the unequal division of wealth and the government of England with the island of Utopia. In Utopia there is little poverty, a better distribution of property, free education for all people, no unemployment, and the good of each person is sacrificed to the common good of the state. We today wonder: If we took religion and meditation as seriously as did Thomas More, might not God's Utopia, the Kingdom of God, almost become a reality?

Martin Luther 1483-1546

A WORLD CONGRESS of Christians was held in Cleveland in the summer of 1931. At one of the evening meetings, T. Z. Koo of China and Toyohiko Kagawa of Japan were the speakers. I shared a hymn sheet with a representative from Norway; next to me sat a person from India. One of the hymns sung that night was *A Mighty Fortress Is Our God,* from the text by Martin Luther. It was printed in English, French and German, and all three languages were simultaneously sung that night by the thousands from all parts of the world. As I heard this vigorous hymn sung in several languages, I said to myself: Surely here is the theme of all mankind, for no language can corral the thought! *A Mighty Fortress Is Our God* is a courageous note which belongs to all races, tongues and centuries! It is at the heart of all great religious living.

This great hymn by Martin Luther was inspired by the words of Psalm 46, in the sixteenth century when Luther was pioneering for the Reformation: "God is our refuge and strength, a very present help in trouble." Called "the sublime song of faith," Psalm 46 was written in a time of Jewish national calamity after the Babylonian exile, showing fearful people that their one source of strength and stability lay in God. In similar fashion James Russell Lowell points men to God as "a mighty fortress":

Though the cause of evil prosper,
Yet 'tis truth alone is strong:
Though her portion be the scaffold,
And upon the throne be wrong,—
Yet that scaffold sways the future,

And behind the dim unknown,
Standeth God within the shadow,
Keeping watch above His own.

At this time in world history, when men are fearing the outcome of western culture, might we become more stable and more courageous persons, with greater wisdom to face our problems, if we put at the heart of our credo: "A mighty fortress is our God!"

At the close of the Edinburgh Conference in 1937, a Lutheran theologian from Europe expressed Martin Luther's note of absolute faith in God in these words to Dean Willard Sperry of Harvard: "We have been speaking about the ethic of Jesus, through the medium of the Church, as the way to make the world the Kingdom of God. If the Kingdom of God ever comes, it will be *entirely* a gift of God!"

Luther wrote numerous hymns, for he felt that the singing of hymns was one of the surest ways to make worshipers aware of God's grace. "I always loved music," he said. "Whoso has skill in this art, is of a good temperament fitted for all things. We should not ordain young men as preachers, unless they have been well exercised in music. The singing of hymns is a goodly thing and pleasing to God. Music is a noble gift of God, next to theology. I would not change my little knowledge of music for a great deal." In 1524 he brought out a hymnbook of twenty-three hymns, of which he was partly the composer and author. Each hymn deeply expresses the heart of Luther's theology. Though a man of vigorous physical dimensions, he nevertheless realized that he was totally dependent upon God's unfailing grace for whatever he might accomplish:

Therefore in God I place my trust,
My own claim denying.
Believe in him alone I must,
On his sole grace relying.
He pledged to me his plighted word.
My comfort is in what I heard.
Therefore will I hold forever.

But Luther not only brought music into the life of the worshiper; he also opened the Bible to those who might find a deeper spiritual nourishment. His German translation of the Bible became a classic example of German literature; it became the open door for salvation to the Protestants in the sixteenth century.

I remember a beautiful September day in 1929 when I traveled from Eisenach, Germany, to Wartburg Castle, where Luther translated the New Testament into the German language. Amidst the Thuringian hills with their gorgeous fall foliage, the castle seemed a place where a scholar would yearn to go, where alone he could transmit his ideas into manuscript. But Luther in 1520 was in no mood for the solitariness of the Wartburg Castle: "I can tell you in this idle solitude there are a thousand battles with Satan. Often I fall and am lifted again by God's right hand. I am mighty displeasing to myself, perhaps because I am alone. I did not want to come here. I wanted to be in the fray. I had rather burn on live coals than rot here." Ill health and insomnia weakened his physical energy. But he did find one cure for his mental depression at The Wartburg–it was in his labor which finished his translation of the New Testament within the period of a single year. "Luther did the work of more than five men," says a recent critic. The Wartburg achievement is a living example of this statement.

In July, 1505, a university student named Martin Luther was struck by a bolt of lightning on a road near the Saxon village of Stotternheim. In his fright he prayed: "St. Anne help me! I will become a monk." Born in Eisleben of a peasant family, Luther studied law at the university in Erfurt. Because of his frightening experience during the storm, and his vow to St. Anne, Luther entered an Augustinian monastery. Ordained to the priesthood in 1507, made vicar of eleven monasteries in 1515, and renowned as a professor of biblical literature at Wittenberg, the monk was to renounce his vows. In 1517 he nailed ninety-five theses on the castle church at Wittenberg. The young man who wished to become a monk had now become a reformer. But throughout his experiences his spiritual life savored of that of a saint, for at the center of his life was the triumphant note, "A mighty fortress is our God!"

John of the Cross 1542-1591

Several years ago, after preaching in a church in Canton, Ohio, I received a letter from a woman who attended the service; she enclosed this poem:

I cannot find the stars tonight,
So black the sky bends over;
I cannot hear the happy winds
That glean the fields of clover.

I cannot see the bladed grass,
So dark the night-tide going;
I cannot hear the happy leaves
Singing their songs of growing.

But somewhere, where the shadows end
Begins a newer story;
And somewhere past horizon's rim
The day is making glory.

And surely in the soundless darks
The honey-saps are flowing;
And somewhere waits the perfect bloom
A gracious Hand's bestowing.

At the conclusion of the poem she wrote, "I do not know poetry, but I do know these verses hold a truth that gives me strength for courageous living." She did not realize that this poem and her comment were looking into what John of the Cross calls "the dark night of the soul." This experience is known as one of the "seven deadly sins," called "sloth." It is a mood in which a person feels dryness of the spirit,

God seems far away, a person condemns and hates himself, he feels alone and does not know where to find power to pull himself together. It is an experience which comes to deeply religious persons. Jeremiah the prophet had it: "Why is my pain perpetual and my wound incurable which refuses to be healed: Wilt Thou be unto me as a deceitful brook, as waters that fail?" Job also knew its hurt: "How long wilt Thou look away from me, nor let me alone till I swallow my spittle?"

John of the Cross was the son of a poor silk-weaver. After elementary school education, he worked for seven years in a hospital; then he attended a Jesuit school and was ordained at twenty-five. In 1658 with Teresa of Avila, a converted dancing girl, he organized the Order of the Barefooted Carmelites, a religious movement which deeply improved the spiritual life of Spain and France. In his classic writing, *The Dark Night of the Soul*, John of the Cross describes the sad loneliness of a person's spirit, and shows how he can overcome this terrifying feeling.

If we feel this inner desolation, John suggests four aids:

1. The first requirement for those who join Alcoholics Anonymous is a willingness to be helped. John of the Cross likewise emphasized one's desire as necessary to get out of the state of depression.

2. The troubled soul must not try too hard to arise above depression. Rather one should at first be quiet, take rest, not be too active. Alternating with this quiet attitude a person should meditate on the life and suffering of Christ.

3. One must accept those experiences which cannot be altered; and locate the causes of those which can be changed.

Selfishness and fear cause much of our spiritual depression and can be remedied; 90 per cent of our fears are about events which never will happen. Most of us are hungry for more self-importance than self-approval can give.

4. One who has a sick soul must get a bigger perspective of life. He should center himself in some life purpose, in other people's needs, in God. His feeling should be like that of the young woman who said, "Life is just too much trouble unless one can live for something big!" John of the Cross saw the wisdom of his Master who once said to his disciples: "If you are my disciples, take up your cross and follow me . . . The greatest of all is a servant . . . He who loses his life for my sake and the gospel's shall find it . . ."

The "dark night of the soul" is an experience which comes to most of us, just as it came to men as diverse as Martin Luther and Robert Louis Stevenson. Luther said, "I am utterly weary of life. I pray the Lord will come forthwith and carry me hence . . . Rather than live forty years more, I would give up my chance of Paradise." Stevenson wrote, "There is indeed one element in human destiny that not blindness itself can deny. Whatever we are intended to do, we are not intended to succeed; failure is the fate allotted." But both of these men—and so can we—through their religious faith were able to rise above their melancholy. Luther continued to write hymns and Stevenson persisted in writing his fascinating tales!

Francis of Sales 1567-1622

FRANCIS OF SALES is not the first person of noble birth to throw away the purple garments of his caste for the cloak of a religious leader. Gotama (the founder of Buddhism), Mahavira (the founder of Jainism), and Isaiah the Old Testament prophet are other dramatic illustrations of noblemen dedicating themselves to God's work.

Born of noble parents at the Castle of Sales near Annecy, France, Francis entered a Jesuit school in Paris. There he studied the classics, Hebrew and philosophy, and led a life of severe self-discipline. Later he studied law at Padua, and at twenty-four was made a doctor of laws. Soon he turned from law to the church and was sent to Switzerland as a missionary. Here he fought Calvin and the reformers with the weapon of Christian love. In 1602 he was made bishop of Geneva, a post he diligently served until his death in 1622.

The classic writing of Francis of Sales, *Introduction to the Devout Life*, is a "primer" for the devotional life. Possibly written for his friend Madame Charmoisy, it proved a guide for her spiritual living, and has also offered excellent suggestions for the last three hundred years. Francis was especially effective in aiding well-to-do and educated persons in their religious development. He seemed to have the knack of making goodness attractive.

Unlike John Calvin who felt that man was depraved, Francis looked upon all men as having potentialities for goodness. "There is no natural temperament so good," he said, "that it may not be made evil by vicious habits; there is no natural temperament so refractory that it may not, first by the Grace of God and then by industry and diligence be subdued and overcome." When man begins to think about God, a new spirit begins to emerge in his breast: "As soon as a man thinks with even a little attention of the divinity, he feels a certain delightful motion of the heart which testifies that God is God of the human heart." Tolstoy shared this viewpoint. The great Russian tells how, after years in which he contemplated suicide, he began to find that whenever he *thought* about God a new release of energy crept into him. After such an experience of God he concluded: "There arose in me, with this thought, glad aspirations toward life. Everything in me awoke and received a meaning . . . To acknowledge God and to live are one and the same thing. God is what life is. Well, then, live, seek God, and there will be no life without him."

As a discipline for the devotional life, Francis laid out a pattern of ten lessons, each to take an hour a day, preferably at an early morning hour. On these ten days were ten successive subjects for meditation: creation of the world, the purpose of our being created, the gifts of God, sin, death, judgment, hell, heaven, choice of heaven, and the choice which the soul makes of the devout life. Through these spiritual meditations, the individual opens the floodgates of his soul so that the seeking mercy of God can enter. A "good" man, according to Francis, abides by God's commandments out of a sense of duty; a "devout" person is heroically good with enthusiasm and warm love.

The pietism of a devout man is not one to be practiced apart from the world, but *in* the world among people. Yet Francis saw the necessity of those who would graduate from being "good" to becoming "devout," to sever their self-indulgence: "Stags when they have put on too much flesh, withdraw and retire into their thickets, knowing that their fat is such a burden to them that they are not fit to run, should they chance to be attacked; so also the heart of man burdening itself with the useless, superfluous and dangerous affections cannot run after God readily, freely and easily which is the true mark of devotion." There is a fatness of the soul, akin to the fatness of the body, which the devout athlete of God must curb through spiritual discipline.

Evening prayer also has great value for Francis. He suggests that before we go to sleep, we thank God for His care over us through the day; that we examine our conduct through the day which is past; that we thank God for any good we have done, and ask His forgiveness for evils performed, with determination to do better on the morrow; that before we fall asleep we commend body and soul, the church, our relations and friends to God; that God keep watch over us through the night.

Religion for Francis was a spiritual banquet, as it was for most of the saints. He saw the place of prayer similar to a garden perfumed by flowers. As we gather a few flowers from a garden to remind us of its beauty, so we carry from the sanctuary a few high points of our meditation, making them into a spiritual nosegay.

Jacob Boehme 1575-1624

CHRISTIAN SAINTS have come from every walk of life; Teresa was a ballet dancer; John Woolman was a tailor; Brother Lawrence was a footman and a soldier; the Apostle Paul was a tentmaker; Thomas More was Counselor to the king; Rulman Merswin was a banker. Jacob Boehme, like most of the saints, came from a common occupation, that of a shoemaker in Silesia. Called "the inspired shoemaker," he was born in the little market town of Alt Seidenberg, of German Lutheran parents. Not formally educated, he found his training through prayer, the Bible and the writings of the Christian saints. "I am only a layman," he once said, "I have not studied, yet I bring to light things which all the High Schools and Universities have been unable to do." Through self-education he became intellectually brilliant. When he was twenty-five, he saw the sunlight reflected one day on a pewter dish. This ordinary experience suggested to him that he too was illumined by the Light of God. He went immediately to the Public Green, and there he seemed to see God illumined in nature. "The gate was opened to God," he said, "and in one quarter of an hour I saw and knew more than if I had been many years in a University."

When fourteen, Jacob Boehme became a shoemaker's apprentice at Seidenberg. One day a poorly dressed man came to the shop to purchase shoes. Jacob Boehme felt incompetent to sell shoes to him; but the buyer persisted in the purchase. Boehme placed the price so high that sale seemed prohibitive; but the man bought them. As the stranger left the shop he said to Boehme, "Jacob, come hither to me. Thou art little, but thou shalt become great—a man very different from the common cast, so that thou shalt be a wonder to the world. Be a good lad; fear God and reverence him." These words left a deep impression on Boehme—he feared God and reverenced Him the rest of his life. After a decade as a traveling cobbler, Jacob Boehme married and set up his own shop in Görlitz.

To read the story of Jacob Boehme is to remember that saints are not necessarily geniuses. They are ordinary persons, deeply devout and heroically good, who are willing to surrender themselves to God's power, love, and wisdom; when they do that, God has an unusual way of magnifying their abilities. Boehme is described by one of his friends in these words, "He was gentle in manner, modest in his words, humble in conduct, patient in suffering and meek of heart. His spirit was highly illuminated of God beyond anything Nature could produce."

"God as Light" describes Boehme's idea of deity; and as this Light had once been revealed in Jesus Christ, so it could enlighten the lives of those who followed the Master. Boehme felt that insights into spiritual truths often came with suddenness. "There are moments," he said, "when the soul sees God as in a flash of lightning . . . I am only a very little spark of God's Light, but He is now pleased in this last time to reveal through me what has been partly concealed from the beginning of the world."

Edwin Markham wrote a poem some years ago, "How the Great Guest Came." This poem depicts a cobbler much like Jacob Boehme. The cobbler had a dream that his Lord was going to visit him in his shoe shop:

"The Lord appeared in a dream to me,
And said, 'I am coming your guest to be. . . .' "
Only the half of him cobbled the shoes,
*The rest was away for the heavenly news.**

The cobbler anxiously awaited his visitor. The door soon opened; it was only a beggar: "He gave him shoes for his bruised feet." The door opened a second time, to have an old woman enter; she was wrinkled and sad, with fagots on her back: "He gave her his loaf, and steadied her load." The third time the door to his shop opened; a pale, thin child entered: "He gave it milk in a waiting cup." By this time the cobbler was restless, wondering if his guest were coming. He cried out:

"Why is it, Lord, that your feet delay?
Did you forget that this was the day?"
Then soft in the silence a Voice he heard:
"Lift up your heart, for I kept my word.
Three times I came to your friendly door,
Three times my shadow was on your floor.
I was the beggar with bruised feet,
I was the woman you gave to eat,
*I was the child on the homeless street!"**

Whether we read about Markham's humble cobbler or look into the heart of Jacob Boehme, we hear Jesus say to all saints who perform simple acts of kindness to those in

* Edwin Markham, "How the Great Guest Came" from *Shoes of Happiness and Other Poems.* Copyright 1915, 1932 by Doubleday, Page and Company. Reprinted by permission of Virgil Markham.

need, "Inasmuch as you have done it unto the least of these, my brethren, you have done it unto me." Through such acts God's Light reflects through us and illumines the way of needy travelers as they grope in the dark along the highway of life.

Lancelot Andrewes 1555-1626

I NEED MORE grief, I plainly need more grief. I am far from that grief which I ought to know. I can sin much, but I cannot repent much. Oh, my dryness and my deadness! Woe unto me! Would that I had more grief or sorrow of heart! But of myself I cannot obtain it. I am dried up like a potsherd. Open in me, O Lord, a fountain of tears. Give me a molten heart." In such contrition of heart cried Lancelot Andrewes, intimate friend of King James I and Francis Bacon. Rare linguist (master of fifteen languages), outstanding preacher, one of the translators of the King James Version of the Bible, bishop of Chichester, Ely and Winchester, Lancelot Andrewes made his greatest contribution to Christianity in his *Private Devotions.* Written for his own use in Greek and Latin, this work became public property at his death. No devotional masterpiece shows more deeply the search of the soul for its counterpart.

"The original manuscript," wrote a friend of Andrewes, "was slubbered with its author's hands and watered with his penitential tears." Said another, "To myself one of the chiefest compensations and off-sets for the reign of King James I is this, that the *Private Devotions* were being continually composed and were being continually employed—were being continually wrung out of him—during the whole course of that so mischievous reign."

In a great and yearning moment Lancelot Andrewes cried to God in an "Act of Pleading":

Remember what my substance is,
dust and ashes,

flesh and a wind that passeth away,
corruption and the worm,
as a stranger and sojourner upon earth,
inhabiting a house of clay,
whose days are few and evil,
today and not tomorrow,
at morning and not until evenings,
now and not presently,
in a body of death,
in a world of corruption,
that lieth in wickedness;
Remember this.

Although written for the time of King James I, this is a penitential prayer for us today. As we, like Lancelot Andrewes, try to be "Christians in an unchristian society," we in our frailty feel our part of the sins of the world and the deep need for God's grace and forgiveness. We find ourselves in a situation similar to that of Louis XVI in the eighteenth century. In writing to George Washington about Louis XVI, Gouverneur Morris, the American representative in Paris, said, "Louis XVI was a good man. In ordinary times he would have made a good king. But he has inherited a revolution." The same might be said about many of us today. In ordinary times, without great problems to meet and solve, we could (without great difficulty) be good persons. But in our civilization we have inherited a revolution, and as this revolution goes on within each of us, we have a hard time getting along with ourselves. Each person is battling against selfishness, fear, resentment and guilt. Before we can renovate the social scene of history, we must first remove the guilt within ourselves.

Pitirim Sorokin, sociologist of Harvard University, paints two types of people in the history of civilization. One type has met famine, war and pestilence with cynicism, despair and bestial living. The other type has risen to heights of great moral behavior and deep devotion to ideals. Sorokin concludes that the diverse reactions to similar situations have been caused by the values for which the different groups have lived. The Jewish-Christian tradition exemplifies a people who have met their trials with triumphant courage and high idealism because they believe God is the center of their life. Like Lancelot Andrewes we need to seek God's help, as through our penitent spirits His mercy, power and wisdom can function. Upon such persons civilization's future must depend!

The prayer, "For the Church of Christ Throughout the World," uttered by Lancelot Andrewes in the early years of his ministry, still breathes today the spirit of the church universal:

"Let us pray for the churches throughout the world, for their truth, unity, and stability; that in all, charity may flourish, and truth may live. For our own Church, that what is lacking in it may be supplied, and what is unsound corrected; for the sake of Jesus Christ, our only Lord and Savior. Amen." If the 650,000,000 Christians throughout the world would utter this prayer with sincerity, and then follow their prayers with social action, wondrous consequences would result!

Blaise Pascal 1623-1662

In June, 1928, when I was leaving America for a year of graduate study in theology in Marburg University, Germany, Bishop Edwin H. Hughes wrote me these friendly words: "Don't let your mind submerge your heart in your theological studies." Blaise Pascal agreed with this beloved bishop, when he wrote: "The heart has its reasons, which reason does not know. We feel it in a thousand things. . . . It is the heart which experiences God, and not reason. This, then, is faith: God is felt by the heart, not by reason." Pascal did not mean that we should exalt the "heart" over the "head," or that we should be unintelligent in our approach to religion. He felt that the whole self—reason and faith—must be involved to know God, with faith outreaching reason. The German philosopher Schleiermacher would add that "religion is man's feeling of absolute dependence upon God."

Pascal did not arrive easily at his faith in God, even though he was reared in a religious atmosphere. Founder of mathematical principles of the cone before he was sixteen, genius in the world of calculus, one of the founders of the science of hydrodynamics, he came to his religious beliefs after disbelief and protest of Christianity. Pascal stayed outside Jansenism, though his family became converts in 1646. In 1653, after study of Montaigne and Epictetus, he sought salvation outside the Christian way. But he found no satisfaction. After visiting his deeply religious sister Jacqueline at Port Royal, and spending two months in serious search of God, he had a profound religious experience on November 22, 1654;

and on January 7, 1655, he went into retreat. His conversion he described on a piece of paper, which thereafter he wore sewn into his coat.

Pascal was neither a philosopher nor a theologian. He was a man of mathematical and scientific inquiry who was intellectually curious about religious issues. He enjoyed the culture of the world, so he could never be purely ascetic. He was "a man of the world among ascetics, and an ascetic among the men of the world; he had the knowledge of worldliness and the passion of asceticism, and in him the two are fused into an individual whole." His life was spent in acts of extravagant asceticism and charity.

Six years after his conversion Pascal compiled notes for a book in defense of the Christian faith. It was never written. After Pascal's death a friend compiled these miscellaneous notes into a volume known as *Pensées* (thoughts). The ideas in his *Pensées* are as valuable today as they were in Pascal's time: "Thought constitutes the greatness of man. . . . If we submit everything to reason, our religion will have no mysterious and supernatural element. If we offend the principles of reason, our religion will be absurd and ridiculous. . . . Faith is a gift of God; do not believe that we said it was a gift of reasoning. . . . The knowledge of God is very far from the love of Him. . . . We must love God only and hate self only. . . . If there is one sole source of everything, there is one sole end of everything; everything through Him, everything for Him. . . . It is an extraordinary blindness to live without investigating what we are; it is a terrible one to live an evil life, while believing in God. . . . Experience makes us see an enormous difference between piety and goodness. . . . None is so happy as a true Christian, nor so reasonable, virtuous, or amiable. . . . The Christian religion makes man altogether lovable and happy. In honesty, we cannot perhaps be altogether lovable and happy. . . . Not only do we know God by Jesus Christ alone, but we know ourselves only by Jesus Christ. Apart from Jesus Christ, we do not know what is our life, nor our death, nor God, nor ourselves."

I have an uncanny feeling that many educated people, who have "thrown away" religion, could find significant and helpful advice from Blaise Pascal. He was able to tie reason and faith together in man's approach to religious truth. As a brilliant though deeply torn genius, he finally found his vision of God. Says T. S. Eliot of him: "I can think of no Christian writer, not even Newman, more to be commended than Pascal to those who doubt, but who have the mind to conceive, and the sensibility to feel, the disorder, the futility, the meaninglessness, the mystery of life and suffering, and who can only find peace through the satisfaction of the whole being."

Jeremy Taylor 1613-1667

JEREMY TAYLOR was born in 1613, the son of a barber, near Cambridge University. When grown to manhood, after winning scholarly fame at Cambridge University, he was to be chaplain to the king, and bishop of Down and Connor. Taylor, never afraid to speak the truth, was imprisoned three times.

Several years ago I found a century-old copy of his *Golden Grove* in a second-hand bookstore. In the preface to this book of devotional instructions, he criticizes the indifference to religion among the church people of his time: "Instead of the excellency of conditions, and constitution of religion, the people are fallen under the harrows and saws of impertinent and ignorant preachers, who think all religion is a sermon, and all sermons ought to be libels against truth and old governors; and expound chapters, that the meaning may never be understood; and pray that they may be thought able to talk, but not to hold their peace; they caring not to obtain any thing but wealth and victory, power and plunder." For this criticism of the church, he was imprisoned in 1654–55!

Jeremy Taylor is one of the great preachers of the Christian centuries. A nineteenth-century writer compared the sermons of his day with Taylor's homilies: "We have no modern sermons in the English language that can be considered as very eloquent. For eloquence we must ascend as high as the days of Jeremy Taylor." To read Taylor's writings is to join in fellowship with a great Christian saint who felt the bigness of the Christian religion.

Marriage was a theme of deep interest to Bishop Taylor:

"Marriage is a school and exercise of virtue . . . marriage is the nursery of heaven . . . it hath in it less of beauty, but more of safety, than the single life; it hath more care, but less danger; it is more merry, and more sad; it is fuller of sorrows, and fuller of joys; it lies under more burdens, but is supported by all the strengths of love and charity, and those burdens are delightful." At a time when there is more than one divorce for each four marriages, the words of Jeremy Taylor need serious attention.

The holy institution of marriage has lost much of its sanction today. The Roman Catholic Church considers it one of the seven sacraments. Unfortunately the Protestant Church retained only two sacraments, the Lord's Supper and baptism. In some ways marriage seems the most sacred rite in religion. If the atmosphere of a home is deeply religious, and children are instructed in spiritual values, the neighborhood, the city, the state and the world are affected. "Marriage is the mother of the world," wrote Taylor, "and preserves kingdoms, and fills cities and churches, and heaven itself . . . marriage, like the useful bee, builds a house, and gathers sweetness from every flower, and labors and unites into societies and republics . . . promotes the interest of mankind, and is that state of good things to which God hath designed the present constitution of the world."

At the heart of the ideal marriage Taylor saw the necessity of sympathetic love: "Let man and wife be careful to stifle little things, that as fast as they spring they be cut down and trod upon; for if they be suffered to grow by numbers, they make the spirit peevish, and the society troublesome, and the affections loose and easy by an habitual adversation. . . . He that loves not his wife and children feeds a lioness at home, and broods a nest of sorrows; and blessing itself cannot make him happy. She that is loved is safe, and he that loves is joyful. The man's authority is love, and the woman's is obedience; for this obedience is no way founded in fear, but in love and reverence."

Marriage is a holy sacrament for Jeremy Taylor, to be entertained only by those of a prayerful mood. In his devotional classic, *Golden Grove*, is a prayer to be used by those entering the marriage state: "And now, O Lord, since by thy dispensation and over-ruling providence, I am to change my condition, and enter into the holy state of marriage, which thou hast blessed by thy word and promises, and raised up to an excellent mystery, that it might represent the union of Christ and his church; be pleased to go along with thy servant in my entering into, and passing through this state, that it may not be a state of temptation nor sorrow, by occasion of my sins or infirmities, but of holiness and comfort, as thou hast intended it to all that love and fear thy holy name. Amen."

Several years ago when I was beginning a book, *The Fellowship of the Saints*, a critic wrote, "Be sure to include materials from Jeremy Taylor, especially from his *Holy Living* and *Holy Dying*." This I did, for Jeremy Taylor has much to say to man's spiritual living and dying in any century. Little did his intelligent barber-father realize that the tutoring of his son in grammar and mathematics was to lay the foundations of a future bishop of the Church of England and a Protestant "saint" of the centuries!

Henry Scougal 1650-1678

FEW MEN have attained greater heights of religious leadership within a span of twenty-eight years than Henry Scougal. Appointed by the bishop professor of divinity at King's College when twenty-three, Scougal was the first professor in Scotland to teach Baconian philosophy. His book, *The Life of God in the Soul of Man*, is looked upon as the classical devotional writing of the Scottish church. In this writing he compares real religion to artificial or secondary religion.

Harry Emerson Fosdick suggests that religion should not be something we try to defend by arguments, but an experience which defends us; that we should not worry about saving religion, for real religion saves us. Henry Scougal agreed, for he wrote: "So few understand what it (religion) means; some place it in the understanding, in orthodox notions and opinions; and all the account they can give of their religion is that they are of this or the other persuasion, and have joined themselves to one of those many sects whereinto Christendom is most unhappily divided. Others place it in the outward man, in a constant course of external duties and a model of performances . . . Others again put all religion in the affections, in rapturous hearts and ecstatic devotion. . . . They know by experience that *true religion* is a union of the soul with God, a real participation of the divine nature, the very image of God drawn upon the soul, or, in the apostle's phrase, it is Christ formed within us."

A modern poet, Grace N. Crowell, catches the value of

Scougal's God-centeredness for the purpose of real religion when she writes:

The Power that holds the planets in their courses,
That places limits on the restless sea,
Holds my life too within its mighty keeping—
Always holds me.

I say this over and over when storms are heavy.
I say it when the night is on the land.
I whisper that behind the Power Almighty
Is God's kind hand.

And so I rest as a swan rests on the river,
Quiet and calm amid life's troubled flow.
I know I am held by a Power and a love
*That never will let go.**

Like the Apostle Paul, Henry Scougal saw Christian love as the "more excellent way." "Love," he said, "is the greatest and most excellent thing we are masters of; and therefore it is folly and baseless to bestow it unworthily: it is, indeed, the only thing we can call our own. Other things may be taken from us by violence, but none can ravish our love." In the spirit of Robert Southwell, Scougal would say, "Not where I breathe, but where I love, I live."

Religious psychologists remind us today that our inner frustrations are caused by self-centeredness which breed inner, subjective fears, animosity and jealousy of others; that 90 per cent of our fears are psychological, rather than

* Grace N. Crowell, "The Great Love" from *The Lifted Lamp*. Copyright 1942 by Harper & Brothers. Reprinted by permission of the publishers.

logical, since we try to revolve the universe with ourselves as the centers of reference. For these mentally ill persons Henry Scougal had a cure: "Why should we entertain such unreasonable fears, which dampen our spirits, and weaken our hands, and augment the difficulties of our way? Let us encourage ourselves with those mighty aids we are to expect in this spiritual warfare; for greater is he that is for us, than all that can rise up against us: 'The eternal God is our refuge' (Deut. 33:27), 'and underneath are the everlasting arms,' 'Let us be strong in the Lord, and in the power of his might' (Eph. 6:10), for he it is that shall 'tread down our enemies' (Ps. 44:5)."

To the statement "Let go and let God" Henry Scougal would gladly assent, for he would call this the secret of courageous, unselfish Christian living. Christianity has always been the most practical of religions, as it has attempted to help people in life situations. Jesus brought peace to his fearful disciples as the stormy sea tossed its waves high about their boat on the sea of Galilee; the Gospel of Mark in similar fashion attempts to bring the peace and power of Jesus' gospel amid Roman persecutions; Jesus' religion today can bring spiritual security to his followers as the waves of daily difficulties toss high around them.

How little times have changed the art of Christian living! There is little difference between seventeenth-century Scotland and twentieth-century America! The words of Jesus sound for us as modern and penetrating as they did for Henry Scougal: "Do not be anxious about your life . . . Look at the birds of the air: they neither sow nor reap nor gather into barns, and yet your heavenly Father feeds them. Are you not of more value than they? Which of you being anxious can add one cubit to his span of life? . . . If God so clothes the grass of the field which today is alive and tomorrow is thrown into the oven, will he not much more clothe you, O you of little faith . . . Seek ye first his kingdom and his righteousness . . . Do not be anxious about tomorrow, for tomorrow will be anxious for itself. Let the day's own trouble be sufficient for the day."

George Fox 1624-1691

A CHRISTIAN SHOULD be radiant. In a Roman prison the Apostle Paul writes to the Philippians, "Rejoice in the Lord always; again I say, Rejoice." Philippe Vernier, a French Protestant, imprisoned in solitary confinement, describes his experience: "I had joy and wonder. God was so near and real that I was sometimes overpowered. There was a song in the depths of my heart. The happiness was like that of a rescued child, as though I were on an ocean all drowned, and then, God's arms underneath me, lifting me up." George Fox in his prison cell said that "he could walk cheerfully over the world." Men like these measure up to the standard of sainthood suggested by Baron von Huegel to Rufus Jones, "A saint must be radiant!" Like all saints George Fox found the secret of power and joy in centering his life in God. "Be staid," he wrote, "in that principle of God in thee, that it may raise thy mind to God—thou wilt find God at hand."

George Fox, the son of a weaver in Leicestershire, England, became a cobbler and a shepherd. At nineteen, after he had been drinking beer with "professors" of the Christian religion, he heard the Lord say, "Thou must forsake all, both young and old, and keep out of all, and be as a stranger unto all." He was discouraged to find that so-called Christians were no different from other people in their daily practices. Leaving his home he wandered about, trying to find aid from preachers for God's guidance. Ministers did not seem prepared to help him. "To be bred at Oxford or Cambridge was not sufficient to fit a man to be a minister of Christ. I regarded the priests less, and looked more after the Dissenting people."

In 1647 Fox became a traveling minister of the gospel, his travels broken at intervals by a total of six years in prison. While imprisoned in Derby, England, in 1650, he and his friends were nicknamed "Quakers," because they made people tremble at the word of God. When in 1666 his health was shattered by his frequent imprisonments, he gave his time less to traveling and more to building up a church order for the Quakers. He also helped some members of Parliament frame ideas for the Toleration Act, which would give them religious freedom. His *Journal*, which records his life events, was edited in 1694 by Ellwood, and was printed verbatim in 1911 by Norman Penney.

William Penn said of George Fox: "He was of an innocent life; no busybody, no self-seeker, neither touchy nor critical . . . so meek, contented, modest, easy, steady, tender, it was a pleasure to be in his company. He exercised no authority, but over evil, and that everywhere and in all; but with love, compassion and long-suffering." The secret of his religious life was found neither in theological doctrines nor in ritualistic forms, but in his close relationship to God's spirit which gave him the guidance of an "inner light." To feel God's spirit within the breast was the secret of religion; it brought man back to the "Tree of Life." "I knew God experimentally," said Fox. "I had the key that doth open. I came up through the flaming sword into the Paradise of God and was in the condition of Adam before he fell."

The religious movement founded by George Fox was called "The Society of Friends." Its members did away with creeds, abandoned the use of water, bread and wine in the sacraments, stressed the use of silence in worship, and encouraged merciful deeds toward their fellow-men. With stress of help for the poor, freedom of thought to every individual, and close communion of God with each human spirit, George Fox speaks a wise word for the present year.

The words of his prayer in 1671 ring true for our present needs: "O Lord God Almighty! Prosper truth, and preserve justice and equity in the land! Bring down all injustice and iniquity, oppression and falsehood, and cruelty and unmercifulness in the land; that mercy and righteousness may flourish! . . . And the Lord in mercy bring down all these things in the nation, to stop thy wrath from coming on the land."

In his last letter in his journal, dated September 25, 1790, to his friends, he confesses the heart of his gospel: "All you that preach the truth, do it as it is in Jesus, in love; and all that are believers in Jesus, and receivers of Him, He gives them power to become the sons of God, and joint-heirs with Christ; whom He calleth brethern; and He gives them the water of life . . . For all that be in Christ are in love, peace, and unity. In Him they are strong."

Brother Lawrence 1611-1691

MANY FIND IT more difficult to worship in a kitchen than before an altar. Some feel themselves serving God better through preaching to crowds than in washing pots and pans. But it was different with Nicholas Herman (called Brother Lawrence): "The time of business," he said, "does not with me differ from the time of prayer; and in the noise and clutter of my kitchen, while several persons are at the same time calling for different things, I possess God in as great tranquillity as if I were upon my knees at the blessed sacrament." It took ten years of careful spiritual discipline before he was able to achieve "the practice of the presence of God" in the duties of daily living.

Brother Lawrence was a soldier and a household servant who became a lay member of the Barefooted Carmelites. Without formal education, outside elegant cathedrals, and void of elegant ritual, he was able to have a personal union of himself and God. This was for him the highest goal of living. "I cannot imagine how religious persons can live satisfied without the practice of the presence of God. For my part, as I can, I keep myself retired within Him in the very center of my soul, and when I am so with Him, I fear no evil." His conversion began at eighteen, when on a midwinter day he saw a leafless tree. As he reflected that spring would soon bring blossoms and leaves to the tree, his thoughts turned to the wonders of God in His world. From that time he endeavored to walk constantly "as in His presence."

We can well imitate Brother Lawrence in seeing our tasks

as sacraments. Almost every labor can be seen as a holy calling; ministers and priests are not the only persons who are "called" to sacred work. Teachers, streetcar motormen, factory employees, bankers, actors, editors, housewives, doctors and farmers can view their work as holy, in which they are using their talents to make this world God's Kingdom. We, like Brother Lawrence, can find God in our daily duties in various ways.

God can be "practiced" in beauty. Henry Ward Beecher felt that he owned every flower in Brooklyn; David Thoreau possessed every bird, squirrel and garden in Concord. The religiously minded person sees the design of the universe pointing to the Designer. A man blind for years, who suddenly recovered his sight, cried out: "O Lord, how great and marvelous are all Thy works!" God can be found in solitude and meditation as depicted in the experience of one who said: "The room was filled with a Presence, and I knew that I was not alone. I belonged and knew I was never again to be afraid." God is found in acts of unselfish moral living, where a person treats his fellow-men with thoughtful love. This was expressed by a college youth on a Christmas eve after giving gifts to a poor tenement family: "God was never closer to me than on that night as I walked down those rickety tenement stairs." God is discovered in a Christian fellowship, where people as "the body of Christ" or the "body of believers" are knit together by the power, wisdom and love of a Christlike God.

The Christian finds God in a carefully balanced life of work, play, love and worship. Like Brother Lawrence he sees "the practice of the presence of God" as the center of his power and joy. For him the suggestions of Brother Lawrence seem contemporary: "I make it my only business to persevere in His holy presence wherein I keep myself by a simple attention and an absorbing passionate regard to God, which I may call an actual presence of God; or to speak better, a silent and secret, constant intercourse of the soul with God, which often causes in me joys and raptures inwardly . . . In short I am assured beyond all doubt that my soul has been with God these past thirty years and more . . . As I apply myself to prayer, I feel my whole spirit lifted up without any trouble or effort of mine; and it remains as it were in elevation, fixed firm in God as in its center and resting place." Like the poet, Brother Lawrence could say:*

So here in the roar of mortal things,
I have a place where my spirit sings,
In the hollow of God's Palm.

* Edwin Markham, "The Place of Peace" from *Shoes of Happiness and Other Poems*. Copyright 1915, 1932 by Doubleday, Page and Company. Reprinted by permission of Virgil Markham.

François Fénelon 1651-1715

SOME YEARS AGO in Akron, Ohio, in the ballroom of the Mayflower Hotel I attended a meeting of the Oxford Group, then commonly called "Buchmanites." On the stage of this room, with a red plush curtain behind them, I heard men in tuxedos and women in evening gowns make their confessions about how God had saved them to the life of a Christian. An advertising expert from New York City was disappointed in science and philosophy in helping him find meaning for life; a Detroit banker was on the verge of divorce; a German countess suffered bitterness and melancholy; an automobile sales manager was fighting alcoholism; a millionaire industrialist was harassed by business worries—but now they were saved from their frustrations into joyful, vigorous living through the help of religion. The Oxford Group Movement purposed to save the "up-and-out" into a higher plane of Christian living.

François Fénelon would have found rapport in this religious group, for being religious was "the thing to do" among well-to-do Frenchmen in his time; and through the sincerity of his efforts he kept a spirit of earnestness in their religious strivings. The son of the Marquis of Fénelon, he was raised in backgrounds of luxury and educated under a private tutor. Of outstanding mind and oratorical ability, he was made a priest at twenty-four and at twenty-seven was given the assignment of instructing women converts of nobility into the Roman Catholic faith. He tutored the Duke of Burgundy so excellently that Louis XIV made Fénelon the archbishop of Cambrai in 1695. When Fénelon later became interested in the mysticism of Madame Guyon, he lost his prestige in court circles.

Evangelism to Christian values is as much needed among the cultured classes as among the "down-and-out." Fénelon sensed this need in his day. We can profit by his practice in our modern world. Persons of powerful ability, lost in their wealth and prestige, need their abilities converted from their self-pride into service for others. Encased in their pride and selfishness, they become problems to themselves and to other people.

At the heart of religion François Fénelon found humility. "The saints," he said, "have all agreed that true humility is the groundwork of every virtue, and that because it is the offspring of pure love, and because humility is truth itself. There are but two truths—the almightiness of God and the nothingness of us his creatures; and if humility is real, it will make us pay continual homage to God through our lowliness, abiding in our proper place, content to be nought." Fénelon felt that perfection lay in never thinking of ourselves, or of the relation in which God stands to us. A saint is one who does not love Christ as *his* Redeemer, but only as *the* Redeemer of the human race, and the more love we have for ourselves the less we can spare for our Maker.

We need to see the difference between humility and an inferiority complex. Such a complex is a vice, a negative attitude toward life, resentment toward others' success. Humility is a virtue, a positive manner of living, in which man as a little creature *feels* himself related to God's majesty and holiness. The shift from pride to absorption in something bigger than ourselves is the secret of changing from the inferiority complex to humility. Two contemporary novelists illustrate the change: One writer describes a woman called Edith who was "a little country bounded on the north, south, east and west—by Edith." Edith was a selfish individual who never graduated from childish selfishness. The other novelist has one of her characters—a young woman struggling to keep her values—say, "Life's just too much trouble unless one can live for something big!" It is this dying from the type of Edith-self and living to the type patterned by the girl who lives for something big which is at the heart of Christian experience.

In an era when the pride of men has brought deterioration into western civilization, the voice of François Fénelon with its stress on humility needs our attention. "Do not test humility by external appearance," he wrote, "by this or the other action, but solely by love. Pure love strips self from off a man, and clothes him with Jesus Christ, so that 'it is no more I that love, but Christ that liveth in me.' "

William Law 1686-1761

A SMALL STURDY man of lively countenance and keen eyes, in his middle fifties, is met by a stranger in the door of a London shop. "Are you, sir, the Reverend William Law?" The stranger places an envelope in Law's hands and loses himself in the crowd. William Law finds a thousand-pound Bank of England note in the envelope. Soon he uses this money to establish a school for fourteen poor children in King Cliffe. Two women friends add their funds to his; with their three thousand pounds they expand the school for poor children, and establish day-by-day help for the poor. Later, Law purchases four cows, whose milk he gives to his needy neighbors. He believes in and lives a social religion.

William Law was born into a prosperous home at King Cliffe, England. After graduating from Emmanuel College, Cambridge University, in 1707, he was ordained in the Church of England and taught at Cambridge. Unable to take the oath of allegiance to King George I, he gave up his orders as a priest and lost his teaching position at Cambridge. In 1727 he became the tutor of Edward Gibbon, who later became the father of the great historian. He spent four years as tutor in the Gibbon family as "the much honored friend and spiritual director of the whole family." When young Gibbon went abroad to study, Law remained another ten years in the Gibbon home as religious guide to its members and their neighbors. John and Charles Wesley came under his religious influence in this period. In 1740 Law inherited his father's estate at King Cliffe; he lived there the rest of his days. In his later years he was deeply influenced by Jacob Boehme, "the inspired shoemaker" of Germany. It is said of Law, "He began as a controversialist and ended as a mystic."

William Law felt his career greatly disturbed when he was forced to abandon the priesthood after his refusal to give allegiance to King George I. During this experience he wrote: "My prospect indeed is melancholy enough, but had I done what was required of me to avoid it, I should have thought my condition much worse. The benefits of my education seem partly at an end, but that same education had been miserably lost if I had not learnt to fear something more than misfortune." He felt that loyalty to Christ should be uncompromising. He was sick of seeing so many half-hearted, half-empty Christians. In the year 1951 he would be dismayed to find that only one fourth of our nominal Christians take any vital attitude in the work of the Church. Most of the people in his day were lukewarm Christians. They were decent people, but they lacked a religious drive. Many needed "a serious call to a devout and holy life," the theme of his religious classic.

We wonder today why people lack the depth and fervor of the first-century Christians. William Law has an answer: "If you will here stop and ask yourselves why you are not as pious as the primitive Christians were, your own heart will tell you, that it is neither through ignorance nor inability, but purely because you never thoroughly intended it." Within each of us lies a "will to believe" and also "a will to become."

Back of the churches' indifference Law saw the dryness of the spiritual lives of its members. They were "dry bones." Their deterioration was caused by their lack of prayer; each member must begin the prayer life anew: "As the morning is to you the beginning of a new life; as God has then given you a new enjoyment of yourself, and a fresh entrance into the world; it is highly proper that your first devotions should be a praise and thanksgiving to God . . . Receive, therefore, every day as a resurrection from death, as a new enjoyment of life; meet every rising sun with such sentiments of God's goodness, as if you had seen it, and all things new created upon your account; and under the sense of so great a blessing, let your joyful heart praise and magnify so good and glorious a Creator."

Law's faith in the value of prayer is expressed in the words of Richard C. Trench:

Lord, what a change within us one short hour
Spent in Thy presence will avail to make!
What heavy burdens from our bosoms take!
What parched grounds refresh as with a shower!
We kneel, and all around us seems to lower;
We rise, and all, the distant and the near,
Stands forth in sunny outline, brave and clear;
We kneel, how weak! we rise, how full of power! . . .

John Woolman 1720-1772

It is August 26, 1758. On this date John Woolman denounces slavery in a public meeting. Some have called this the birth of our present-day social conscience in America.

John Woolman was born in Burlington County, New Jersey, of Quaker parents, in a home where with his six brothers and six sisters he was taught the value of industry, frugality and spiritual quiet. Though lacking in much formal education, his *Journal* mentions his private reading of such books as *Don Quixote*, Milton's *Paradise Lost*, Thomas More's *Utopia*, and the writings of Eusebius, Erasmus and Jacob Boehme. Only a person with deep intellectual yearnings would pursue such volumes. At one time he was a schoolmaster; he prepared legal documents for his friends and compiled a school grammar. His major time, however, was given to tailoring, when at twenty-one he started his trade in a Mt. Holly, New Jersey, tailor shop. Within seven years he owned the shop.

John Woolman might have become wealthy at tailoring or at other lucrative businesses, but he saw the evil in attaining too much wealth. His *Journal* records this warning: "Such Buildings, Furniture, Food, and Raiment, as best answer our Necessities, and are the least likely to feed that selfish Spirit which is our Enemy, are the most acceptable to us. In this State the Mind is tender, and inwardly watchful, that the Love of Gain draw us not into any Business, which may weaken our Love to our Heavenly Father, or bring unnecessary Trouble to any of his Creatures." He often advised poor people to buy less expensive goods from him, thus lessening his profits. "A life so plain that a little suffices" was the motive of Woolman.

Fourteen years after John Woolman's public denunciation of slavery in New Jersey, he set out for England. King George III had sent a message to the governor of Virginia to do away with any attempts to interfere with the slave trade in his colony. Earlier in his *Journal*, after travels in Virginia and North Carolina, John Woolman wrote, "When I ate, drank, and lodged free cost with people who lived in ease on the hard labor of their slaves, I felt uneasy . . . I saw in these southern provinces so many vices and corruptions increased by this trade and this way of life that it appeared to me as a dark gloominess hanging over the land." In his journeys among those who held slaves in New Jersey, Pennsylvania and New England, Woolman traveled by foot instead of on horse, that he might feel more deeply the weariness of slaves. He refused to use sugar, molasses and dyes imported from the West Indies, where slave labor was employed.

The Negro problem is still turbulent in American life. Several years ago the tragedy of being a Negro in America was revealed by a Negro girl who won a prize in an essay contest: "How Should We Punish Adolf Hitler?" She said that the worst punishment would be to give him a black skin and force him to live in the United States the rest of his life. Recent figures from eleven states show that we spend an average of $44 per white student in the public schools, only $12.50 on each Negro student; we have one hospital bed for each 150 white people, but one hospital bed for each

2,000 Negroes, among whom sickness status and death rate are worse than among white people.

Progress has been made in racial understanding in the last few years. Negro students are being admitted to colleges and universities; big league baseball has welcomed such players as Jackie Robinson, Satchel Paige, Larry Doby, Luke Easter; interracial churches exist. Yet we have a long distance to go in bettering racial relations. A Christian symbol of what interfaith and interracial unity ought to be in America was beautifully portrayed at a Good Friday service, 1939, in Washington, D. C., as Marian Anderson sang *Ave Maria* standing by the Lincoln memorial. There stood a Negro Protestant woman singing a Roman Catholic aria in praise of a Jewish woman, Mary, the mother of Jesus. How John Woolman would have loved that scene! By 1771 almost all of the Societies of Friends in America had stopped the use of slaves, largely due to Woolman's influence.

While John Woolman was in England on his mission to curb the sanction of slavery, he fell ill of smallpox. On October 7, 1772, he died of the disease, in spite of the loving care given him by Friends. The words of Jesus seem to fit the career of John Woolman: "The greatest of all is a servant." Woolman was a living incarnation of his own words: "To keep a watchful eye towards real Objects of Charity, to visit the Poor in their lonesome Dwelling-places, to comfort them who, through Dispensations of divine Providence, are in strait and painful Circumstances in this Life, and steadily to endeavor to honor God with our Substance, from a real Sense of the Love of Christ influencing our Minds thereto, is more likely to bring a Blessing to our Children, and will afford more Satisfaction to a Christian favored with Plenty, than an earnest Desire to collect much Wealth to leave behind us . . . My heart was often tendered under the divine influence and enlarged love toward the people among whom we traveled."

John Wesley 1703-1791

It is May 24, 1738, in an Aldersgate Meeting House in London. The minister is reading Luther's *Commentary on Romans*. Among the listeners John Wesley, an Anglican priest, is deeply affected: "About a quarter before nine, while he (Luther) was describing the change which God works in the heart through faith in Christ, I felt my heart strangely warmed. I felt I did trust in Christ, Christ alone for salvation; and an assurance was given me, that He had taken away my sins, even mine, and saved me from the law of sin and death." Eight years before this experience, John Wesley with his friends at Oxford had formed a "Holy Club." Because these young men were so "methodical" in their daily religious habits they were nicknamed the "Methodists." The conversion of John Wesley at the Aldersgate Meeting House was the beginning of the Methodist movement.

Organized religion in England in the time of Wesley was cold and lifeless; drunkenness and morality were at their worst in English history. The working classes lacked spiritual leadership, the upper-class churches were noted for their empty pews. John Wesley's preaching was directed to the working classes, often to thousands in the open fields before the working day began. John Wesley did not intend to break with the Church of England, but since many churches were closed to the enthusiasm of this new religious movement, he was forced to speak to "societies."

Lecky the historian remarks that Wesley, by evangelizing the common people of eighteenth-century England, saved that country from a revolution similar to that in France. At the heart of this revival, which touched the common man, was the idea that man through love of God and neighbor should strive toward "Christian perfection." Many in Wesley's day were critical of his high standard; many today feel it an impossible goal.

More than twenty years ago, when I was ordained to the Christian ministry, the bishop said to the candidates: "Are you going on to perfection?" In the crowded church that fall Sunday afternoon, there was a smile on the faces of some of the people as the required answer was given: "I am earnestly striving for it." But this is no laughing matter, for unless we who are Christians are striving for perfection, then we are missing the mark of Christianity. "Be ye therefore perfect even as your Father which is in heaven is perfect," said Jesus, and he meant it. The quest for perfection is at the core of purposive living.

I recently listened on a Saturday afternoon to Wagner's *Tristan und Isolde*. When I heard "Liebestod" from that opera, I said, "If I could but create something as perfect as that, I should feel as if I had accomplished my life purpose." Then I remembered that Wagner composed *Tristan und Isolde* in 1857; and that after this composition came *Siegfried*, *Die Götterdämmerung*, *Der Ring des Nibelungen*, *Die Meistersinger*, *Parsifal*. "Be ye perfect" seemed the motivation for Wagner's creative work. Paderewski on concert tour needed the discipline of daily practice. If he missed one day of practice, he felt his playing was inferior; if he missed two days, he was sure the critics detected the difference; if he missed three days, he knew his audience felt something was wrong with his artistry. "Be ye therefore perfect" was the attraction for Paderewski's concert work.

Each day is a time for us to look into ourselves and see where we need perfecting and cleansing. Wesley wrote in his day: "Be patterns to all of denying yourselves, and taking up your cross daily. Let them see that you make no account of any pleasure which does not bring you nearer to God, nor regard any pain which does; that you simply aim at pleasing him, whether by doing or suffering; that the constant language of your heart, with regard to pleasure or pain, honor or dishonor, riches or poverty, is:

All's alike to me, so I
In my Lord may live and die!"

Each day is a time for us to be perfect!

On April 2, 1739, Wesley began his evangelism when he preached to three thousand sooty miners in a brickyard at Bristol. Today more than eight million persons are members of the church which he began. Wesley's Aldersgate conversion experience bore results.

John Frederic Oberlin 1740-1826

In July, 1960 my wife and I visited the home of John Frederic Oberlin in Waldbach. The excellent roads which led to this Alsatian village were built by Pastor Oberlin in the early days of his ministry. These highways were symbolic of other things done by Oberlin—they were lasting. And to think that the villagers of Waldbach threatened to do physical harm to Oberlin because he innovated new roads!

Few lives are more dramatic or intriguing than that of Oberlin: Minister for over fifty years in the Alsatian parish of Waldbach, he materially and spiritually transformed a rocky, barren, war-devastated area around Ban de la Roche. He introduced weaving, cotton-ginning, straw-plaiting; he rebuilt roads; he founded schools; he taught Jews, Roman Catholics and Protestants to worship together. Two great disciplines were basic for Pastor Oberlin's success—prayer and tithing.

As a man of deep spirituality, he frequently dismounted from his horse outside the little village of Ban de la Roche, and there on his knees, with tears streaming down his cheeks, prayed for the needy people of his parish. Each morning for an hour he knelt in devotions in his study, interceding for his parishioners. As they walked past the parsonage with bowed heads and hushed voices, they knew it was a sacred hour in that Alsatian village.

Pastor Oberlin was deeply concerned for his parishioners. In a questionnaire of twenty suggestions he asked: "Do you never pass a Sunday without employing yourself in some charitable work? Are you careful to provide yourself with clean and suitable work? Are you careful to provide yourself with clean and suitable clothes for going to church in on the Sunday? Have your civil and ecclesiastical overseers reason to be satisfied with your conduct, and that of other members of your family? Are you frugal in the use of wood? Do you keep a dog unless there be absolute necessity? Do you so love and reverence your Lord and Savior, Jesus Christ, as to feel united in the bonds of Christian fellowship with that flock of which he is the pastor?" Religion touched every bit of life!

For his tithing Pastor Oberlin used three boxes. The first was a deposit for the worship of God—"for building and repairing of churches and schoolrooms; the support of conductrices; the purchase of Bibles and pious books; in short, anything connected with divine worship." The second tithe box was for useful purposes, for improvements of the roads to churches and schools; for teachers' salaries; for Sunday dinners for poor people; for expenses incurred in becoming a godfather; for churchwardens; for repairing injuries. The third box was used for the poor: "I devote the contents of this box to the service of the poor; to the compensation of losses occasioned by fire; to wood flannel and bread, for those who stand in need."

Pastor Oberlin devised a way by which he would always have money to help needy causes: "When I cannot pay ready money all at once, I mark how much I owe upon a bit of paper, which I put into the box; and when, on the contrary, a demand occurs which ought to be defrayed by one of the three allotments, and there is not sufficient money deposited, I advance the sum, and make the box my debtor, by marking upon it how much it owes me. By this means I am always able to assist in any public or charitable undertaking; and as God has himself declared, 'it is more blessed to give than to receive.'"

John Frederic Oberlin was decorated with both the ribbon of the Legion of Honor and the gold medal from the French Agricultural Society. His highest honor, however, was the saintly esteem placed upon him by his parish. In a letter to his friends who paid him honor on his seventieth birthday, he wrote: "The beautiful flowers with which your great Creator adorned our country, gave you the means of presenting me with this testimony of your united love. These flowers will very soon fade, but the impression they have made upon my heart will never die, and I earnestly pray that you may become unfading flowers in the Paradise of God."

A contemporary writer speaks of Pastor Oberlin: "He was a Protestant saint whose life is one of the best illustrations in human history of greatness achieved through fidelity to a despised and neglected field of work." Was it not through prayer and tithing that God used him to such great advantage for the kingdom? The God of Pastor Oberlin is still the God of history in 1951—and prayer and tithing are still instruments by which God can use us for His high purpose!

One never knows where the results of the devoted Christian life will spread. Seven years after the death of Pastor Oberlin, in 1833, a college was established in Ohio by the Reverend John J. Shipherd and Mr. Philo P. Stewart. Its purpose was "to train teachers and other Christian leaders for the boundless and most delicate fields in the West." Inspired by the saintly life of Pastor Oberlin of Waldbach, they called this institution Oberlin College.

William Ellery Channing 1780-1842

In October, 1842, the chimes of the Catholic Cathedral in Boston toll as the funeral procession of William Ellery Channing passes slowly through the streets. Today in the Boston Public Garden stands a monument with these words engraved to Channing's memory: "He Breathed into Theology a Humane Spirit." Channing has been called the "lay saint" of modern times. After his visit to England, Coleridge said of him, "He has the love of wisdom, and the wisdom of love. He is the very rarest character on earth."

William Ellery Channing is called the father of Unitarianism. In 1819 he went to Baltimore, Maryland, to preach at the ordination of Jared Sparks. What he said then is considered the stimulus for the Unitarian movement in the United States. In 1825 the American Unitarian Association was formed with Channing as its recognized leader, with Ralph Waldo Emerson and Theodore Parker his close friends in this liberal movement. Channing, however, never liked the word "unitarian," for he felt that it was as abstract as the word "trinitarian." Broad in his religious views, he saw little difference between unitarians and trinitarians. He did, however, favor the unitarian view because he felt it was supported in the Bible.

In 1812 Channing called Calvinism "a curse," because it viewed man as depraved and unable to choose salvation. Channing was a champion of the spiritual and intellectual freedom of man; he stressed "a Christianity which is liberal, kindly, gentle and considerate in its judgment of those who may differ." The resurrection of Christ was, he remarked, "a fact which comes to me with a certainty I find in few ancient histories."

As champion of the social gospel, Channing in 1816 led to the organization of the Massachusetts Peace Society. After a visit to the West Indies, his book *Slavery* in 1835 had the thesis, "Man cannot be justly held and used as property." Yet he felt that the emancipation of slaves should come by the educated conscience rather than by legislation. A sermon, "Religion, a Social Principle," caused the omitting of a compulsory tax for the support of religious worship.

A visitor today at Arlington Street Church, Boston, can see the graceful pulpit used by Channing in his Federal Street Congregational Church, where he preached for over forty years. It stands as a shrine of simple beauty to a man who consecrated his life to reason, humanity and the power of the spirit. Though he was short and slight, he had large eyes and a wonderfully clear voice, and spoke with simplicity and grace of style. A friend of his once described him thus: "Dr. Channing small and weak! I thought him six feet at least, with fresh cheeks and broad chest, a voice like that of many waters and strong-limbed as a giant!" Spiritually, Channing was a giant, though his earlier life of a recluse with its self-denials had left him with a weakened body. Before he was twenty, he passed through a spiritual battle. About this struggle he wrote, "I cannot find a friend with whom I can converse on religious struggles." To another he said, "I was worn well nigh to a skeleton." Although this experience wrecked his health, it brought Channing intellectual victory in his religious thinking.

Behind the life of this saintly person lay a life of daily prayer: "The Scriptures of the Old and New Testaments agree in enjoining prayer. Let no man call himself a Christian who lives without giving a part of life to this duty." He recommends the morning prayer: "In the morning our minds are not so much shaken by worldly cares and pleasures as in other parts of the day. Retirement and sleep have helped to allay the violence of our feelings, to calm feverish excitement so often produced by intercourse with men." But the evening is equally of value for spiritual reflection: "This season, like the morning, is calm and quiet. Our labors are ended. The bustle of life has gone by. The distracting glare of the day has vanished. The darkness which surrounds us favors seriousness, composure and solemnity . . . The evening is the time to review not only our blessings, but our actions . . . The hours of activity having passed, we are soon to sink into insensibility and sleep. How fit that we resign ourselves to the care of that Being who never sleeps, to whom the darkness is as the light, and whose providence is our only safety."

Daily prayer for us, as for Channing, can change our lives from a stage of worry into a stage of wonder, from dull daily routine into wondrous adventure, from self-centeredness into social concern for mankind!

Many of us can profit greatly from the social creed of Dr. Channing: "To live content with small means; to seek elegance rather than luxury, and refinement rather than fashion; to be worthy, not respectable, and wealthy, not rich; to study hard, think quietly, talk gently, act frankly;

to listen to stars and birds, to babes and sages, with open hearts; to bear all cheerfully, do all bravely, await occasions, hurry never. In a word, to let the spiritual, unbidden and unconscious, grow up through the common. This is to be my symphony."

F. August Tholuck 1799-1877

THERE COMES A midnight hour when all men must unmask," said the Danish theologian, Sören Kierkegaard. With this "midnight hour" of death August Tholuck was deeply concerned: "As for thee, man, who has never yet made peace with God, how can he possibly be happy in this life, seeing that every moment is conducting him farther and farther away from the place which contains all that gives pleasure to his heart? Every tick of the clock, every particle of sand that drops in the hourglass, proclaims that a fragment of his life, and with it, of his fortitude and joy is gone."

The pietism of August Tholuck savors of depth of living and height of thinking. For over fifty years he taught at Halle University, Germany, the center of rationalism. Here as a defender of evangelical Christianity, opposed by faculty colleagues, he became successful in tying reason and pietism together; what he did changed the whole character of the seminary at Halle. Before his death, Tholuck was considered one of the foremost preachers and most beloved "saints" in the Protestant world.

The Christian seriously considers the meaning of death. Thoughtfully he reflects: "The Christian is to live forever. So is everyone else, but the Christian knows it. The result is that he is deprived of the consolation of a tidy view of the world."* In similar vein, August Tholuck caught a

* Chad Walsh, *Stop, Look and Listen.* Copyright 1947 by Harper & Brothers.

glimpse into every person's occasional thoughts about the mystery of death: "I am confident that there is not a human being whose heart has not, some time or other, felt a presentiment of the terrors of judgment. No one believes that all is over at death, or at least believes it firmly and at all times. And will not what is to ensue thereafter merely resume the thread which was broken here; and if so, will there be no accusers to testify of hours misspent, of privileges abused, of places profaned, of debts unpaid and hidden secrets of inquiry?"

But because Tholuck looked from time into eternity through Christian eyes he could further say: "O my soul! is it indeed the case that no man can be happy in this life without the assurances of salvation in the life to come? Be it then thy endeavor so to live as at the hour of death thou wilt wish to have lived. While time lasts, lay hold on eternity. Above all, lay hold on Him who has said, 'Whosoever believeth on me hath everlasting life.'"

During World War II, as I sat at my study desk on a December afternoon, I caught the spirit of August Tholuck and his thoughts about life and death. This is what I wrote:

The snowflakes are falling patiently and kindly, lodging securely on the boughs of the campus trees. . . . Through the soft curtain of snow I discern the spire of the college chapel pointing upward as though to direct my thoughts to God. . . . The sight of the chapel reminds me of the 1,600 students who have walked in and out of its doors, now on the fighting fronts of the world. . . . I realize that death to many of them at this very moment is imminent. . . . I try to parallel their thoughts of death with mine. . . . I conclude that many of them are weighing death in terms of moments, hours, days; I am weighing my death in terms of years. That is the difference. I want to live my life as courageously and dynamically in the years that lie ahead as they are forced under the expediency of war to live their lives in these tragic days . . . The thought of death deepens my desire to live! . . . I arise from my chair and say to myself, "I am not afraid of death; I believe that death is necessary in order to enrich life!"

On that day the century of Tholuck spoke an inspiring thought to my high hour of contemplation about death! I felt as though I had an answer to Tholuck's question: "Is death the sleep which no dreams disturb? Is it the dark partition between us and the holy land? Is the swift moment, the little bridge on which the brief sleep of time encounters the long awakening of eternity?"

Death is a part of the totality of experience; it is never to be isolated as something separate from life; it is synonymous with selfless living. Proper thought of death should be constructive; it should urge a person to live his life with every degree of intensity. It creates in him a mood so beautifully expressed by the poet, Clyde Tull:

Afraid to live? Nay, I would grow,
Triumph, conquer, fail, forego;
Not one whit of pain or bliss
In this Earth-life would I miss.
Life is marvelously good,
Full of Love and Brotherhood.
Afraid to die? Nay, Death to me
Would wondrous fine adventure be.

·F. AUGUST THOLUCK·

Beyond the narrow bounds of Sense
I would gain experience.
What care I for mould'ring sod–
Death would bring me nearer God!*

* Clyde Tull, "Afraid." Reprinted by permission of the author.

George Matheson 1842-1906

To FIND GOD in our sorrows seems the test of a great soul. George Matheson was one of these saintly persons who used his sorrows to deepen his religious living. Blinded totally at twenty years of age, he was determined to prepare himself for the Christian ministry. In spite of his blindness, he earned three degrees at Glasgow in the four years following the loss of his vision. Later he received honorary degrees from Edinburgh and Aberdeen universities. Prepared to speak about "the power of God in sorrow," here is what this great Scottish theologian and preacher writes: "My soul, if thou wouldst be enlarged into human sympathy, thou must be narrowed into the limits of human suffering; Joseph's dungeon is the road to Joseph's throne. . . . It is the shadows of thy life that are the real fulfillment of thy dreams of glory. Murmur not at the shadows; they are better revelations than thy dreams. Say not that the shades of the prison-house have fettered thee; thy fetters are wings—wings of flight into the bosom of humanity. The door of thy prison-house is a door into the heart of the universe. God has enlarged thee by the binding of sorrow's chains."

A beloved bishop once said, "Few people reach the age of forty without having their hearts broken several times." The longer we live, the more we find the truth in these words! Our broken hearts can affect us in different ways: if we have no abiding religious philosophy, sorrow and tragedy can make us cynical, bitter, bestial; if our lives are tied with a Christian viewpoint into the heart of God, our disappointments and heartaches can not only *teach* us something but *make* us something as well. George Matheson belonged in this second group, for he found "strength for the hour" in God: "My soul, why art thou perplexed about the future? Seest thou clouds in tomorrow's sky which thy present strength is inadequate to meet? God has not given thee thy present strength to meet the future, but to meet the present. When thy morrow shall become thy day thou shalt learn thy power over it. Why art thou distressed about the unborn sorrow? Thou thyself art born anew for each new day. Thine armor is freshly burnished to fight each rising sun. In the hour of battle thou wilt laugh at the memory of thy fears."

Like every great saint, George Matheson's life was centered in God, especially in the moments of religious solitude: "It is only when I am alone with Thee that I perfectly understand Thee . . . My soul is within my experience, and I would be alone with it and with Thee. I cannot read the plan of this big world, but I can read the plan of my own life. My sorrows are a mystery to my brother as his are to me, but each of us in his heart has the mystery made manifest. My heart indicates the dark places of Thy providence. Thou hast revealed the parable in my solitude soul. . . . I will not be afraid, though the earth be removed and the hills shaken with the swelling seas, for Thou hast taught me in the lone silence of my spirit the exposition of the great parable—the ark of the flood."

In one of his great moments of surrender to God's will, he penned these words of a well-known hymn, which show the secret of his spiritual power:

Make me a captive, Lord,
And then I shall be free;

Force me to render up my sword,
And I shall conqueror be.
I sink in life's alarms
When by myself I stand;
Imprison me within Thine arms,
And strong shall be my hand.

My will is not my own
Till Thou hast made it Thine;
If it would reach a monarch's throne
It must its crown resign;
It only stands unbent
Amid the clashing strife,
When on Thy bosom it has leant
And found in Thee its life.

On June 6, 1882, the day of his sister's marriage, an unusual experience came to George Matheson: "Something happened to me, which was known only to myself, and which caused me the most severe mental suffering. The hymn was the fruit of that suffering . . . The whole work was completed in five minutes." The hymn to which he refers contains these wonderful lines:

O love that wilt not let me go,
I rest my weary soul in Thee;
I give Thee back the life I owe,
That in Thine ocean depths its flow
May richer, fuller be.

Is not this kind of relationship to God the secret of all

saints of every race and creed, whether ancient or modern? Is not unselfish love in the human heart the one quality which ties all men into oneness with God and brotherhood with one another?

Washington Gladden 1836-1918

For thirty-two years (1882–1904) a dynamic preacher, Washington Gladden, served the First Congregational Church in Columbus, Ohio. He saw religion as an aid to man in meeting his personal problems; but he felt that the test of a personal religion lay within its social and political applications. He was active in helping employers and employees to agree on industrial problems. Though criticized for his liberal views, he was revered by most people. Notre Dame bestowed an honorary doctorate upon him because of his concern for mankind. Born in 1836, and graduated from Williams College in 1859, he gave the rest of his years to the Congregational ministry. He was also on the editorial staffs of the New York *Independent* and *Sunday Afternoon.* Washington Gladden will be best remembered for his hymn: *O Master Let Me Walk with Thee.*

In 1879 Dr. Gladden wrote three eight-line stanzas for *Sunday Afternoon;* it appeared under the devotional section, "The Still Hour," and was entitled "Walking with God." While being maligned by his opponents for his liberal social views, the second stanza of the poem was written as an answer to the mean remarks of his critics:

O Master, let me walk with thee
Before the taunting Pharisee;
Help me to bear the sting of spite,
The hate of men who hide thy light,
The sore distrust of souls sincere
Who cannot read thy judgments clear,

The dullness of the multitude
Who dimly guess that thou art good.

"Dr. Charles H. Richards found the poem," wrote Washington Gladden, "and made a hymn of it by omitting the second stanza, which was not suitable for devotional purposes. It had no liturgical purpose and no theological significance, but it was an honest cry of human need, of the need of divine companionship." With other stanzas added, the poem became the favorite hymn of American Protestantism.

The desire for religious certainty lies deep within most people. Dr. Gladden was no exception. During the mature years of his ministry, he felt some of his theological ideas insufficient. But he knew that Christianity was more than belief in a set of doctrines. Jesus had said to his followers: "You are my disciples if you love me, not because you believe a certain creed about me." In his mental turmoil Washington Gladden realized that he could still live the Christian faith. Out of this experience he wrote these lines:

I know that right is right,
That it is not good to lie;
That love is better than spite,
And a neighbor than a spy.

In the darkest night of the year
When the stars have all gone out,
That courage is better than fear,
And faith is truer than doubt.

The combination of praying, living the moral life and thinking honestly about religious ideas forms a balance to guide us to a creed of deeper meaning.

Twenty years after his famous hymn, *O Master Let Me Walk with Thee,* Dr. Gladden at sixty-one unfolded in a hymn the secret of the guiding power of God in his ministry:

Shine forth, O Light, that we may see
With hearts all unafraid,
The meaning and the mystery
Of things that Thou hast made;
Shine forth, and let the darkling past,
Beneath Thy beam grow bright;
Shine forth, and touch the future vast
With Thine untroubled light.

Washington Gladden stressed social helpfulness to fellowmen rather than dogmas. "Service and not sanctification is, as we have seen, the supreme object of the Christian's desire and endeavor. 'To serve the present age,' this is his high calling." Never discouraged about God's Kingdom coming on earth, he expressed his hope in one of his last sermons: "I have never doubted that the kingdom I have always prayed for is coming; that the gospel I have always preached is true. I believe that the democracy is getting a new heart and a new spirit, that the nation is being saved." He was a living example of the words of his great hymn:

Teach me thy patience; still with thee
In closer dearer company,
In work that keeps faith sweet and strong,
In trust that triumphs over wrong.

How greatly we need the patience, the trust, the social passion of Washington Gladden in our religion today! We need to remind ourselves that God is never to be defeated.

Walter Rauschenbusch 1861-1918

WALTER RAUSCHENBUSCH died in the spring of 1918. Several months before his death, he wrote *The Postern Gate:**

In the castle of my soul,
Is a little postern gate,
Whereat, when I enter,
I am in the presence of God.
In a moment, in the turning of a thought,
I am where God is.
This is a fact. . . .

In this world my days are few
And full of trouble.
I strive and have not;
I seek and find not;
I ask and learn not.
Its joys are so fleeting,
Its pains so enduring,
I am in doubt if life be worth living.
When I enter into God,
All life has a meaning. . . .

The man behind this significant poem is called "Modern Father of the Social Gospel." Like Francis of Assisi, he loved men rather than humanity, and was concerned that the strong should help bear the burdens of the weak.

Born in Rochester, New York, Rauschenbusch's early education was received in Germany; in America he gradu-

* Dores Robinson Sharpe, *Walter Rauschenbusch.* Copyright 1942 by The Macmillan Company. Reprinted by permission of the publishers.

ated from both the University of Rochester and Rochester Theological Seminary. He was ordained in the Baptist ministry. From 1886 to 1897 he helped German immigrants in New York City with their social and religious problems; from 1897 until 1902 he concentrated his efforts to educate German ministers in this country; from 1902 until his death he taught church history at Rochester Theological Seminary. His religious stress was that of the Hebrew prophets and Jesus, that a person cannot be religious unless he practices social righteousness among his fellow-men. His message was much like that of Rabbi Hillel (40 B.C.-A.D. 10) who saw religion in these terms: "What is hateful to thee, do not unto thy fellow-men; this is the whole Law; the rest is mere commentary." He agreed with Jesus: "You shall love your neighbor as yourself" goes hand-in-hand with "You shall love the Lord your God with all your heart, and with all your soul, and with all your mind, and with all your strength."

Walter Rauschenbusch was no fanatic who felt political reform or social change a substitute for religion. Occasionally in America some ministers who preach the "social gospel," and are ousted from pulpits for their liberalism, are confused in believing that you can better America by continuously criticizing her wealth distribution, racial prejudice, attitudes toward war and peace and the liquor traffic. They fail to realize that individuals must first be changed before they can change society. Others feel that Christianity deals only with individual salvation. A friend of mine recently visited a theological seminary where Negroes were not allowed to study for the Christian ministry, and where the faculty was grossly underpaid. At this seminary one of the students said to my friend: "But you must admit that individuals on this campus are full of the Holy Spirit!" Professor Rauschenbusch saw the test of individuals "full of the Holy Spirit" in their social attitudes: "This consciousness of God which we derive from Jesus is able to establish centers of spiritual strength and peace which help to break the free sweep of evil in the social life. Jesus set love into the center of the spiritual universe, and all life is illuminated from that center. . . . Salvation must turn us from a life centered on ourselves toward a life going out toward God and Man." In his social gospel he saw:

There's Asia on the avenue,
And Europe on the street,
And Africa goes plodding by
*Beneath my window-seat.**

James Russell Lowell once wrote: "There is dynamite enough in the New Testament, if illegitimately applied, to blow all our existing institutions to atoms." Dr. Rauschenbusch, however, wanted to use this power constructively: "Humanity is waiting for a revolutionary Christianity which will call the world evil and change it. We do not want 'to blow all our existing institutions to atoms,' but we do want to remold every one of them. A tank of gasoline can blow a car sky-high in a single explosion, or push it to the top of a hill in a perpetual succession of little explosions." The betterment of the world could be done through men becoming changed, as "little puffs" which go out and change their environment.

Like the seers and saints of any age, Walter Rauschenbusch saw the Christian rooted in prayer; prayer made men

* Morris Abel Beer, "Manhattan." Reprinted from *The Book of Poetry* edited by Edwin Markham. Copyright 1927 by William H. Wise and Company.

different: "Men can be classified in many ways. You can classify them as rich and poor, as strong and weak, as capable and stupid, as moral and immoral. But perhaps one of the profoundest classifications would be the division of mankind into men who truly pray and men who do not. There is a great difference between them, both for their personal happiness and for their influence and power in life."

Shortly before his death, Walter Rauschenbusch left his "instructions in case of death": "I leave my love to those of my friends whose souls have never grown dark against me, I forgive the others and hate no man. For my errors and weaknesses I hope to be forgiven by my fellows. I had long prayed God not to let me be stranded in a lonesome and useless old age, and if this is the meaning of my present illness, I shall take it as a loving mercy of God toward his servant. . . . The only pang is to part from my loved ones, and no longer to be able to stand by them and smooth their way. For the rest I go gladly, for I have carried a heavy handicap for thirty years and have worked hard."

Like Jesus, whom he gladly served, Walter Rauschenbusch lived his gospel when he faced death.

Friedrich von Huegel 1852-1925

It is 1907. An Irish priest, George Tyrrell, is excommunicated for criticizing the Roman Catholic Church's idea of hell. In a moment of discouragement he writes to his friend Baron von Huegel, "What a relief if one could conscientiously wash one's hands of the whole concern! But then there is that Strange Man upon His Cross who drives one back again and again." Von Huegel writes Tyrrell twenty-seven letters, and it is through the correspondence of these two friends that we gather many insights into the spirit of Baron von Huegel. "I can most truthfully declare," said von Huegel to Tyrrell, "that no day passes, but you are at least thrice in my prayers." Few men of this century have combined the devotional and the intellectual so beautifully as Baron von Huegel. A loyal member of the Roman Catholic Church, he had sympathy for all seekers after religious truth, but felt that the Roman Catholic Church possessed the richest and fullest interpretation of religious experience.

Friedrich von Huegel was an aristocrat. Son of a foreign minister of Austria, he was privately tutored in Italy, Belgium and England, being equally at home in English, Italian, French and German languages. When a young man, an illness of typhus left him with a weak body and deafness. He was able through much of his life to write but three or four hours a day. While his deafness was in some ways a handicap, it let him live deeply in his quiet interior world. Though a brilliant conversationalist, he was really a silent man who spent much time in meditating on the deepest things of life. In a letter he reminds Tyrrell of the importance of prayer as the secret of being able to meet the hard problems of daily living. "Remember the importance of having one's poor inner world to keep in order whilst fighting a larger and different world outside."

At eighteen years of age, after his father's death, von Huegel spent a year in religious studies at Vienna with a Dutch Dominican friar, Hocking. His father's death, coupled with ill health from typhus fever, shifted his rose-colored world into a place of despair. Friar Hocking led von Huegel into a new perspective of life, by showing him that growth in virtue, service to God and love of Christ come by slow steady plodding. He was told that there are moments when spiritual desolation and dark despair must be faced; that while a person's religion cannot eliminate trials and suffering, it can help him to meet them triumphantly. Such a view greatly aided von Huegel to overcome his own handicaps.

Bishop Alfred Quayle, a Methodist bishop, tells of his experience one night, as he lay awake worrying about a problem. God spoke to the bishop: "Quayle, you go to sleep! I'll stay up the rest of the night and work on the problem!" Baron von Huegel shared the bishop's attitude, and often quoted the words of Bernard of Clairvaux to illustrate his point: "Do you awake? Well, He, too, is awake. If you rise in the nighttime, if you anticipate to your utmost your earliest, you will already find Him waking—you will never anticipate His own awakeness." Ever aware of God's presence, he said: "God not only loves us more and better than we can ever love ourselves, but God loved us before we loved, or could love, Him."

A recent study gives the four major reasons for being religious: religion brings meaning to a person's life; it brings help in time of trouble; it causes a person to treat his fellow-men with sympathy and help; it leads a thoughtful person to believe in God as the Supreme Spirit of the universe. Religion held all of these values for Baron von Huegel: "I should not be physically alive at this moment; I should be, were I alive at all, a corrupt or at least an incredibly unhappy, bitter, self-occupied, destructive soul were it not for religion. . . . Without religion, I should have been unbearable–I needed it to water me down!"

"Christianity taught us to care. Caring is the greatest thing in the world, caring is all that matters," he said shortly before his death in 1925.

He had deep insight into the problem of suffering: "How wonderful it is, is it not, that literally only Christianity has taught us the true peace and function of suffering . . . Christ came and He did not really explain it; He did far more. He met it, willed it, transformed it, and He taught us how to do all this, or rather He himself does it within us, if we do not hinder His all-healing hands. . . . In suffering we are very near to God." Baron von Huegel was able to understand the words of his friend Tyrrell: "There is always that Strange Man upon His Cross who drives one back again and again."

Sundar Singh 1889-1933

Sundar singh is the most spiritual person I have ever known, said Canon Streeter of Oxford. Singh, however, came to this spiritual serenity and power through a hard, long struggle. Born into a wealthy Sikh family in India, he was reared on the *Bhagavad-Gita* and other Hindu scriptures under a deeply reverent mother. Later he was tutored two or three hours a day by a Hindu teacher. But he seemed unsatisfied; he was hungering for inner peace. His spiritual teacher said to him: "If this hunger is not satisfied in this life it will be satisfied in your next rebirths, provided that you keep on trying for it."

He was attracted to the Christian gospel of love after attending an American Presbyterian Mission school and a government school. Later repelled by it, he tore up a Gospel and burned it in the presence of his father. Yet he could not help but see the futile efforts of men seeking salvation in Hinduism. In India he saw a man lying on beds of spikes, another holding his hand up to wither it, another in quietude for six years—each trying to find salvation, but without success. The man on the bed of spikes said: "I worship God in this way, but I confess that the pricks of these spikes are not so bad as the pain I get from my sins and evil desires. My object is to crush the desires of self that I may gain salvation. . . . I began this eighteen months ago, but I have not yet gained my object, nor is it possible to do it in so short a time. Many years, and indeed many births, will be necessary to accomplish it."

Then Sundar Singh told him how he had found salvation

through Christianity in this life: "Though I had done a good deed in burning the Gospel, yet my unrest of heart increased, and for two days after that I was very miserable. On the third day, when I felt I could bear it no longer, I got up at three in the morning, and after bathing, I prayed that if there was a God at all He would reveal Himself to me, and show me the way of salvation and end this unrest of my soul. I firmly made up my mind that, if this prayer were not answered, I would before daylight go down to the railway, and place my head on the line before the incoming train. I remained till about half-past four praying and waiting and expecting to see Krishna, or Buddha, or some other *Avatar* (deity) of the Hindu religion; they appeared not, but a light was shining in the room. I opened the door to see where it came from, but all was dark outside. I returned inside, and the light increased in intensity and took the form of a globe above the ground, and in this light there appeared, not the form I expected, but the Living Christ whom I had counted as dead. To all eternity I shall never forget His glorious and loving face, nor the few words which He spoke: 'Why do you persecute me? See, I have died on the Cross for you and for the whole world.' These words were burned into my heart as by lightning, and I fell on the ground before Him. My heart was filled with inexpressible joy and peace, and my whole life changed. Then the old Sundar Singh died and a new Sundar Singh, to serve the living Christ, was born . . . If, in this present birth, you cannot be successful, then what proof have you that you will gain it in any future birth? Now, not because I am in any way worthy, or have any right, but by His grace and mercy I have been freed from the pricks of sin, and evil desires and temptations, and have yielded myself up to

Him who can take away not only my sins, but the sins of the whole world. For as the spikes have pierced the hands and feet of that Sinless One on behalf of sinners, so now—by His sacrifice—we are saved from sin and its consequences."*

Sundar Singh's conversion was similar to Paul's on the Damascus Road. As Paul suddenly changed from the Law to Christ, so Sundar Singh shifted from Hinduism to Christ, for the secret of a new power, peace and wisdom in daily living. Few may have such a dramatic conversion as his; their Christian religious growth will be slow and gradual. Nor will they have visions like the one shared by Sundar Singh. That Singh found conversion into Christianity, however, is not to be questioned: the test of this change of heart is found in his becoming "the most spiritual person I have ever known," as expressed by Streeter. The feeling of his inner change of heart is echoed in Singh's own words: "Without Christ I was like a fish out of water. With Christ I am in the ocean of Love, and while in the world, am in heaven. For all this, to Him be praise and glory and thanksgiving for ever."*

As we listen to the words of Sundar Singh we say to ourselves: "Strange, yet wonderful, what the Christian faith can do to the spiritual life of man!"

* Sadhu Singh, *With and Without Christ* (London: Cassell & Company, 1929).

Rudolf Otto 1869-1938

I REMEMBER CLEARLY the first time I met Rudolf Otto. I was sitting on the front seat of a lecture room at Marburg University. As he entered the lecture hall from a side door near the front of the auditorium, a shuffle of feet from four hundred students welcomed him to his first lecture on "Ethics," after a sabbatical year in India. He was six feet four inches in height, erect, with a delicate white complexion tinged by pink cheeks; he had a short white pompadour; he was immaculately dressed. The next spring—in May, 1929—when he retired as professor of philosophy of religion at Marburg University, amid much pomp and honors, the active career of a great religious teacher of Germany came to an end. One could feel the greatness of Rudolf Otto; he had a gentleness, a humility, a brilliance and friendliness characteristic of giant personalities.

Born in Germany, educated at the universities at Erlangen and Göttingen, Rudolf Otto taught at the universities of Göttingen and Breslau before coming to Marburg University in 1917. When he finished his university studies in 1897, his religious thinking was unique; hence it was necessary for him through his writings to establish his religious viewpoint. He labored for fourteen years as a "Privatdocent" (somewhat similar to "Instructor" in American colleges), before his interpretations of religion were recognized. With the publication of his great book, *The Idea of the Holy* in 1917 (*Das Heilige*), the world soon recognized a great religious thinker. This book went through many reprints, and was translated into English, Swedish, Japanese, Italian and Spanish.

When I think of a brilliant man like Rudolf Otto disciplining himself for twenty years before writing his major work, I am reminded of Canon William Sanday's words to a class at Christ Church College, Oxford University: "Young men," he said, "I want you to realize that three-fourths of the intellectual work you will do will be sheer drudgery. It will take all the discipline you can muster. But if you can face this fact, you will find that out of the other one-fourth of your intellectual labors, where you do something unique, you will find the joy of intellectual effort." On the spring day in May, 1929, when Otto's students and colleagues paid him high recognition, Otto knew the rewarding joy of creative work, especially central in *The Idea of the Holy*.

Rudolf Otto's view is this: The idea of God's holiness usually indicates God's perfect goodness. But holiness means more than that, as it also signifies God's majesty, bigness, magnificence, infinity. God is the eternal Spirit of this infinite universe whom man holds in awe. By contrast, man in his humility feels his littleness as a creature living on this tiny planet for a few decades. Since God is so great and we are so small, we must "feel" his greatness, for our little minds can never figure out the infinite bigness of God.

A few years ago I read *Dreams of an Astronomer* by Camille Flammarion, in which he tells of going to Mars (37,000,000 miles away), and then to Neptune (2,500,000,000 miles away), then to the nearest light-star, Alpha Centauri (24,000,000,000 miles away), and then out into infinite space, on and on and on, where he finally learned that our little second-rate planet, related to a second-rate sun, is but a tiny room in a solar mansion. Then as I thought of God's Spirit as related to every area in this infinite universe, the littleness of myself overwhelmed me; I felt my humility–I understood what the holiness of God really means–I understood what Rudolf Otto was talking about.

Centuries ago, about 540 B.C., Second Isaiah, one of the greatest of the Old Testament prophets, was trying to convince the Jewish people in Babylonian exile of the holiness of God. He likened the nations of the world to tiny specks of dust or grains of sand, when compared to the bigness of God. One July afternoon in 1949 I sat on the shore of Lake Michigan. I had been reading this illustration from Second Isaiah. As I let the grains of sand sift casually through my fingers, I realized what the prophet Isaiah and Rudolf Otto were saying. I felt sure that too many people today use God as a title, without realizing how wonderful, how great, how powerful the God of the universe really is; and that our religious reformation today must begin by enlarging our thoughts about the God whom we worship and serve.

In Paris in September, 1715, the funeral service of Louis XIV was held in the Cathedral of Notre Dame. After the funeral ritual was performed, the preacher of the court went to the pulpit, where the eulogy was read. As the crowd in the cathedral awaited the eulogy with hushed silence, the preacher said four words: "Only–God–is–great!" That is what Rudolf Otto was saying in *The Idea of the Holy*. We need to remember those words today.

Burnett H. Streeter 1874-1939

CANON STREETER looked like a saint. I heard him speak in 1926 in a Boston chapel. His voice was rather soft; he wore a medium-heavy white beard; his words were carefully chosen and colorful; his eyes possessed a kindly twinkle. Known as both a religious philosopher and a critic of the New Testament, he was deeply concerned with tying the religious values of the New Testament into contemporary devotional living. After his education at King's College School, London, and Oxford, he became a teacher at Oxford, and also acted as canon of Hereford (1915–1934). He was a world citizen of religion, and did much to unite those of the east and the west in their religions.

Biblical scholars have done much to make the Bible intelligible to its readers. Through laboring over manuscripts, digging in archaeological fields, finding clear interpretations of its ideas, making improved translations of the text, these men have brought the Bible to life for many people. Canon Streeter made gigantic contributions to the understanding of the New Testament. Especially in his labors on the Synoptic Gospels (*Matthew*, *Mark*, *Luke*) he discovered four major written documents from which the gospels of Luke and Matthew borrowed. He also suggested that in the New Testament writings seven major theological interpretations about Jesus can be discerned, since Jesus was too great to be captured by a single religious viewpoint. Canon Streeter loved his New Testament, and he wanted to help others appreciate its spiritual values. He felt with another scholar these sentiments about the New Testament:

To love it you must know it;
To know it you must love it.

The gospels in the New Testament are composed of historical facts, coupled with spiritual interpretations, about Jesus. Hence, as we read these gospels today, we should expect to find more than facts within their pages. Canon Streeter stressed the fact that a study of the gospels is a devotional exercise, for the gospels speak spiritually to those who open themselves to their spiritual depth. We can know Jesus by the historical facts in the gospels; but we can also know who he is as we open ourselves to his spirit as portrayed in the New Testament.

Canon Streeter would agree with Albert Schweitzer's words about the way to understand Jesus today: "He comes to us as One unknown, without a name as of old, by the lakeside, He comes to those who knew Him not. He speaks to us the same word: 'Follow thou me!' and sets us to the tasks which He has to fulfill for our time. He commands. And to those who obey Him, whether they be wise or simple, He will reveal Himself in the toils, the conflicts, the sufferings which they shall pass through in His fellowship, and, as an ineffable mystery, they shall learn in their own experience who He is."*

Shirley Jackson Case once said: "Jesus is the enigma of the centuries. What to make of him is a problem to both the saint and the skeptic." A recent anthology on Jesus shows views about him by persons as different as Martin Luther and Oscar Wilde, Pope Pius IX and John Haynes Holmes, Francis C. Burkitt and Napoleon; yet all of these persons view Jesus with high appreciation.

* Albert Schweitzer, *The Quest of the Historical Jesus*. Copyright 1910 by The Macmillan Company.

For Streeter, Jesus was "the ideal man." He would agree that "Christ is the greatest character in history, just as Hamlet is the greatest character in art." Yet he views Jesus also as "the mirror of the infinite": "Christ forces us to face this issue: unless God is at least as good as Christ, then man is nobler than his Creator." It is the way that Christ's love shows us God's love that he reflects the Reality of God.

The New Testament can speak to our contemporary needs if we read its books in the proper mood. Jesus leaps across the changing centuries, because he speaks to the unchanging needs of men and women. To get the most from the New Testament, a person should be alone; he should read its pages slowly and seriously; he should let its suggestions speak to his innermost needs; he should disagree with interpretations if he feels them erroneous; he should listen for the spirit of God and the spirit of Christ behind the words of the writers. After a person reads the New Testament and has found it a panacea or help for his spiritual needs, he should then go out and live its spirit among his fellow-men.

Canon Streeter was a man who not only studied the New Testament scientifically and devotionally; he also lived its precepts in a practical way. On one of his last visits to the United States, before he met tragic death in an airplane accident, he was in an eastern city on Good Friday. He spent the entire day in his hotel room, fasting, praying and reading *The Imitation of Christ.* Apparently his profound study of the New Testament had shown him how to use the results of its pages.

Charles F. Andrews 1871-1940

FELLOWSHIP WITH a great book is often a life-changing experience. Oliver Wendell Holmes discovered that Samuel Johnson was born in 1709; Holmes' birth was in 1809. He thereby decided that he would follow Boswell's *Life of Johnson* in his own time, to see what inspiration he could obtain from his great friend of a previous century. Year by year, month by month he held fellowship with Samuel Johnson. Dr. Johnson died on December 13, 1784. In Holmes' journal we find these words on December 13, 1884: "A hundred years ago this day died the admirable and ever remembered Dr. Samuel Johnson. I feel lonely now that my great companion and friend of so many years has left me." A great book and a great man had left an indelible mark on Dr. Holmes.

A great person and his book likewise made a deep impression on Charles F. Andrews, Christian missionary to India and South Africa. At a time when Dr. Andrews was troubled in his thoughts about the life of Jesus, he read *The Quest of the Historical Jesus* by Albert Schweitzer. Dr. Schweitzer greatly aided Charles Andrews' thinking in saying that Christ was not just a first-century Palestinian person, but "an imperious ruler demanding the soul's allegiance," known by those who do his will. Andrews said, "Schweitzer brought me back to the living Christ, to the Christ I had known and loved in the best moments of my life. He lives on in the hearts of men." The inspiring life of Schweitzer, dedicated unselfishly to the needs of the Negroes in the Lambaréné Forest in French Equatorial Africa, drove Andrews "back to the crucial suffering among the poor and to the homes of the meek and lowly" in India.

Born and educated in India, Charles Andrews joined Tagore in 1913 in India, and from 1923 to 1927 he was in South Africa to help with the Indo-African agreement between India and South Africa. During his many years in India, Andrews was a close friend of Mahatma Gandhi. "When I was actively engaged in trying to help Mahatma Gandhi," he writes, "I was subconsciously occupied in thinking out the spiritual meaning of his personality—so entirely 'Hindu,' and yet so supremely 'Christian.' . . . When I saw Mahatma Gandhi and his followers instinctively taking the true Christian position—suffering wrong-doing patiently and overcoming evil by good—it made me relate, as I had never fully done before, the Law of Compassion which the Buddha taught in India with the Law of Universal Love in Christ." Dr. Andrews' contacts in India made him realize that God's love and forgiveness are found by those of all religions who treat their fellow-men with compassion.

Shortly before his death Andrews said: "The only success that has been worth anything at all has followed closely on those morning hours, which were begun with quiet prayer and silence; when Christ was with me and I listened to His voice leading me forth and giving me His boundless friendship." As a young man working among the poor of South London, Dr. Andrews felt that the way to follow Christ was to spend each day in ceaseless activity, begrudging any time spent in quietude and prayer. Going to India at thirty-four, he learned the value of meditation from the Indians, especially from Rabindranath Tagore, the great religious seer. "I used to watch him and see how different he was from what I was myself. Sometimes when I got up in the night, before daybreak, I would see Tagore already seated in quiet meditation. He would remain there, silent, in the moonlight, very, very early—perhaps two or three hours before the day's work began. So I said to myself, 'Here is something I must learn. I must come to Christ and ask Him to teach me.' "

Those who "take time to be holy" in the hours at dawn seem to find a secret for efficiency throughout the day. Several summers ago I visited Tuskegee Institute in Alabama. In one large room were the scientific discoveries, the lace work, the paintings by George Washington Carver. Each morning Carver arose at four o'clock; he would go into the woods, not only to gather specimens for his laboratory work for that day, but to sit in silence to find how God could use him during that day as His channel of activity in the laboratory. Dr. Carver worked quietly with God in finding the chemical secrets of the peanut and the sweet potato.

Charles Andrews, his life patterned in worship akin to Gandhi, Tagore, Schweitzer and Carver, knew the value of these words:

Keep me quiet, Master,
Patient day by day,
When I would go faster,
Teach me Thy delay.

Restless, oft I borrow
From the future care.
Teach me that to-morrow
Shall its burden bear.

From Thy full provision
Daily richly fed,
By Thy clearer vision
Ever safely led,

Let me to my brothers
Turn a face serene,
Sharing thus with others
Peace from the Unseen.

Evelyn Underhill 1875-1941

By the mercy of God, *Practical Mysticism* came into my hands at a time of great need. It was given to me at the first Christmas of the Great War, in 1914. I had been prepared for its message by many years of searching without finding, and it spoke straight to the heart of my condition. So admits Lumsden Barkway, Bishop of St. Andrews, about one of the earlier of Evelyn Underhill's thirty-three books. Miss Underhill is recognized as one of the outstanding woman writers in the field of religion in the twentieth century. Educated at King's College for Women, London, she became in 1922 the first woman to be a listed lecturer at Oxford University, the first woman to become a Fellow of King's College, London, and one of the few women to be a Doctor of Divinity of the University of Aberdeen. She had the three necessary intellectual virtues in a large degree—"curiosity, candor and care."

The word "mysticism" is misunderstood by many. A few years ago I heard a minister from England preach in Trinity (Episcopal) Church in Boston, whose pulpit Phillips Brooks made famous in the latter part of the nineteenth century. As I left the church, I heard a woman remark: "They say that he is a mystic!" I gathered from the tone of her voice that a "mystic" was something of a spiritual curiosity. I once had a colleague on a college faculty who taught psychology, who referred to odd or unreasonable ideas as "mystical." "Mysticism," however, is not an oddity or a mystery, but a term in religion which indicates that man has a warm and immediate feeling of God's Spirit. It means that as a person breathes air into his lungs, so also a person "breathes" the spirit of God into his spirit. "Mysticism" believes that while study of God is important, the test of our study is, "Do we experience God in our lives?"

Paul Claudel once wrote a letter to a doubter: "A man who wants to know the psychological effects of brandy will find out more by drinking three glasses than by reading all the psychological treatises on the subject in existence." And so it is with "mysticism." Experience of God will tell us more about Him than all the books we can find in a theological library.

The "mysticism" of Evelyn Underhill is very different from the mysticism of Hinduism. The Hindu practices Yoga, the "yoking" of himself to the Spirit in the universe, in order to get away from the practical problems in the world. As the Hindu sits on his crossed legs, with his eyes looking at his nose, he says to himself, "Om–Om–," which means, "I am part of the World Spirit–I am part of the World Spirit." He wants to feel unity with the World Spirit, and thus avoid the ethical problems out in the world. Evelyn Underhill uses a homely illustration to describe her type of mysticism: Here is a garden of flowers which is dry; the garden needs water, else the flowers will die. The gardener fills his watering-can with water, pours the water on the flowers; they take on life, thus growing into bloom and fragrance. In a similar way, she declares, the mystic allows himself to become "filled" with God's Spirit; and once "full" of God's Spirit of power, love and wisdom, he pours out this Spirit on his fellow-men. Thus their lives are bettered, because he has become an instrument of God's Spirit.

As I write presently in my study, an electric light throws its reflective energy upon my desk, not by what the globe and wires do by themselves, but by the energy they receive from a dynamo to which they are attached. Similarly man does not possess the Spirit of God, merely by lifting himself by his own bootstraps or by reading books on God, but rather by his normal relationship to the energy, love and wisdom of God in the universe. Emerson said that by holding a straw parallel to the Gulf Stream the ocean will flow through it. In similar fashion as a person comes into parallelism with God's Spirit, the Divine will flow through it. Such an idea is central in Evelyn Underhill's understanding of mysticism.

Evelyn Underhill views the minister's first task as that of making his parishioners aware of the majestic presence of God in their lives. While committee meetings, administration, parish calling, and community betterment are essential in a minister's work, they are secondary to his making his parishioners aware of "mysticism." Perhaps our churches lack vitality today because they have not heeded advice such as Miss Underhill gives; they have not put first things first. *Fortune* magazine ten years ago said in an article on religion, "Unless the Church makes us hear a voice not our own, we shall all perish." Evelyn Underhill's mysticism is desirous that each of us hear that "voice not our own," the Voice of God, and then do the will of God among our fellow-men.

Thomas R. Kelly 1893-1941

FEW MEN IN recent times have left such an impression of radiant sainthood as Thomas Kelly. After his sudden death Gerald Heard wrote to a mutual friend: "I was filled with a kind of joy when I read of Thomas Kelly. It was formerly the custom of the Winston-Salem community of Moravians, in North Carolina, to announce the passing of a member by the playing of three chorales by the church band from the top of the church tower. So I feel I want to sing when I hear of such men emerging."

Born of Quaker parents in Ohio and educated at Haverford and Harvard, Kelly was called to Haverford in 1936 to teach in the department of philosophy. In 1917–18 he worked with German prisoners in England; in 1924–25 he guided the activities of the Quaker community in Berlin, Germany. In 1941, in the midst of an active life, he died of a heart attack. After his death, five of his devotional addresses, published under the title, *A Testament of Devotion*, give deep and beautiful insights into his spirit.

Rufus Jones tells of Thomas Kelly as he came to him at the end of his first day at Haverford. With his face lighted up with radiance he said to Rufus Jones: "I am just going to make my life a miracle!" The words in one of his essays show the secret of his spirituality: "Placed in coveted surroundings, recipients of honors, we count them as refuse, as nothing, utterly nothing. Placed in the shadows, we are happy to pick up a straw for the love of God. No task is so small as to distress us, no honor so great as to turn our heads." His religious writings remind us that "No life is brief which does perfection win."

In an essay called "Holy Obedience" Thomas Kelly says that many of us have become dull in our religious living; we have lost enthusiasm for the Christian gospel. Meister Eckhart describes us: "There are plenty to follow our Lord halfway, but not the other half. They will give up possessions, friends and honors, but it touches them too closely to disown themselves." The cure for this "halfway" dull kind of religion is through holy obedience to God—we must get away from selfishness and immerse ourselves in God.

Dr. William Burnham has said that until a child is eight years of age, his business is to be selfish, but after that period he must get away from self-centeredness, else he will never be a maturely integrated personality. Today our hospitals and asylums are filled with people who have carelessly become inflated egoists. The superintendent of an asylum in Ibsen's *Peer Gynt* vividly describes this selfish evil in the inmates:

Beside themselves? Oh no, you're wrong.
It's here that men are most themselves—
Themselves and nothing but themselves—
Sailing with outspread sails of self.
Each shuts himself in a cask of self,
The cask stopped with a bung of self,
And seasoned in a well of self.
None has a tear for others' woes
Or cares what any other thinks.

Holy obedience to God puts God at the center of our living, so that each gets away from his "cask of self." Holy obedience, however, asks that we enter into suffering if we are to know God. Sharing the suffering of those in need, we not only find God but we stretch our tiny hearts. "The way of holy obedience leads out from the heart of God and extends through the Valley of the Shadow," Kelly wrote. "God, out of the pattern of His own heart, has planted the Cross along the road of holy obedience. And He enacts in the hearts of those He loves the miracle of willingness to welcome suffering and to know it for what it is—the final seal of His gracious love."

Christian saints have always considered the way of suffering for others as a pathway to God. Caspar René Gregory is a classical example. In 1846 he was born in Philadelphia, Pennsylvania. He went to Germany for study, and there he remained to become a famous New Testament critic at Leipzig University. He tied Christian ethics into the needs of the laboring man in Germany. One rainy night, they tell of him, he saw a streetcar switchman working in the chilly rain. Dr. Gregory went to the man and told him he would watch the switch while the switchman went into the café for a cup of hot coffee. When World I came, Dr. Gregory—then sixty-eight—enlisted in the German army in noncombatant service because he wanted to share the lot of the workingman. In 1916 Gregory was killed in France by a shell. Says Martin Dibelius: "Caspar René Gregory was indeed an illustration of the word: 'Greater love has no man than this, that a man lay down his life for his friend.' "

Thomas Kelly would agree with Gregory that suffering for others is a pathway to God. It is at the heart of Christian living!

Rufus M. Jones 1863-1948

SEVERAL YEARS ago a prominent Quaker of New England said to Rufus Jones, "You must write one more book that will help the college-trained persons who have the scientific outlook to find their way back to a vital religion. They will not accept any interpretation of religion which is inconsistent with that their minds hold as established truth. Hosts of youth that I know have stopped going to church because what they hear is at sharp variance with what they know." Rufus Jones accepted the challenge and in 1948 wrote *A Call to What Is Vital.* Several months after its publication, Rufus Jones passed away. During the past half century, Rufus Jones wrote fifty-four books, all of them concerned with "what is vital" in religion. Born of Quaker parents in Maine, and educated at Haverford, Heidelberg, Harvard and Oxford, he taught philosophy at his alma mater, Haverford College, during the entirety of his career. Honored by degrees from thirteen universities, Rufus Jones was one of America's finest representatives of great religion.

When a boy of nine, the beautiful village in which Rufus Jones lived was almost entirely burned to the ground. He remembers the roaring flames consuming stores and log houses, and how he watched with anxiety to see whether the fire would destroy his home on the edge of the town. That night as he walked along the roads and gazed at the smoldering houses and empty cellars, he felt that something had gone out of his life, never to return. He saw how transitory and uncertain things held so important could be destroyed in a few minutes.

Many owe Rufus Jones a great debt in helping them to realize the closeness of God in human experience. He describes the Spirit of God as close about us as the air we breathe; we have never been separated from the Spirit of God. Even though we have not been aware of God's Spirit which is "closer than breathing, nearer than hands and feet," God's Spirit has nevertheless been around us, keeping watch over us all the time. The purpose of religion is to make us aware of God's presence.

Jones views various ways by which a God of goodness, beauty and truth may become consciously experienced in the life of man; prayer, however, leads man to the mountaintop of his spiritual adventure. Through music, poetry, drama, reflection, friendships, merciful deeds toward our fellow-men—as well as through prayer—can the presence of God be practiced. A girl coming from a symphony of music is described by a poet as being "a little taller than when she went"; an American theologian came into his first great awareness of God as he saw John Drinkwater's *Abraham Lincoln* enacted in a New York theatre; Emily Dickinson viewed the appreciation of literature, especially poetry, as an experience which takes us "up" the mountain trail, when she says:

There is no frigate like a book
To take us lands away,
Nor any coursers like a page
Of prancing poetry.

Beautiful experiences make us aware of a God of beauty!

There are those, such as scientists, who contemplate God through truth. God cannot be seen in the test tube or in the atom by the instruments of scientists, but occasionally a scientist in his work does emerge into a moment of religious exaltation. The astronomical physicist, as he looks a billion light years into the universe, occasionally has the experience of the psalmist:

When I consider thy heavens, the work of thy fingers,
The moon and the stars, which thou hast ordained;
What is man, that thou art mindful of him?
And the son of man, that thou visitest him?

The reverent scientist, as he contemplates the mystery of cell life in his laboratory, sometimes feels with Walt Whitman that "a mouse is miracle enough to stagger sextillions of infidels." The tiny cell and the vast universe bring to man at least an awesome awareness of God as a designer!

To others "the presence of God" is most deeply felt in acts of redemptive kindness among men. It is they who best understand Jesus' words: "Blessed are the merciful, for they shall obtain mercy." Yet through prayer is man's highest experience of God given. Prayer tones one in his total appreciation of God. Rufus Jones portrays man's experience of God through prayer as similar to that of a person climbing Mount Everest: "At first there are many ways which gradually converge, and up to a certain point there are many ways to travel (via beauty, truth, goodness), but at the very last for the final climb there is only one way up (via prayer)... The mystic has been there, and he comes to tell us that beyond all conjectures and inferences about the reality of God is the consciousness of enjoying His presence."*

"Have a sense of what is vital," the Apostle Paul wrote to the Philippians. Rufus Jones' writings help us understand Paul's suggestion.

* Rufus Jones, *A Preface to Prayer.*

Albert Schweitzer 1875-

In the summer of 1949 Albert Schweitzer was greeted by friends in Grand Central Station, New York City. As he and his hosts walked through the station, he spied an elderly woman lugging her traveling bags. Immediately he went over and carried her bags for her to a taxicab. Instinctively his "reverence for life" prompted him to perform this act of service. He remarks about one who accepts the "reverence for life" viewpoint: "Existence will thereby become harder for him in every respect than it would if he lived for himself, but at the same time will be richer, more beautiful and happier. It will become, instead of mere living, a real experience of life."*

Authority on Bach, skillful organist, medical missionary in the Lambaréné Forest, and New Testament critic, Schweitzer well deserves the title of "a modern saint." One of the world's most brilliant men, he has dedicated his talents to the alleviation of human suffering. He was born in Kaysersberg, Alsace, educated at Berlin and Strasbourg, and taught at the latter university from 1901 to 1912. He was organist of the Société J. S. Bach of Paris. In 1913 he became missionary surgeon and founder of a hospital at Lambaréné, Gabon, French Equatorial Africa, where he is still active.

One sometimes wonders why Dr. Schweitzer gave up a university teaching position at Strasbourg, along with his musical career, to go as a medical missionary to Africa. Here is part of his answer: "How did it come about? I read about the physical miseries of the natives in the virgin forests; I

* Albert Schweitzer, *Out of My Life and Thought.*

had heard about them from missionaries, and the more I thought about it the stranger it seemed to me that we Europeans trouble ourselves so little about the great humanitarian task which offers itself to us in far-off lands. The two or three hundred doctors whom the European States maintain as medical officers in the colonial world could undertake only a very small part of the huge task. Society in general must recognize this work of humanity to be its task."

Albert Schweitzer invites everyone to think carefully about religion: "Christianity cannot take the place of thinking, but it must be founded on it," he says. "I know that I myself owe it to thinking that I was able to retain my faith in religion and Christianity." Yet thinking alone will not prove Christianity; our thoughts must be supplemented by living Christian love among our fellow-men. "All living knowledge of God rests upon this foundation: that we experience Him in our lives as Will-to-Love."

The Christian possesses two kinds of love. One is a selfish love for experiences which better him; the beauty he receives from hearing a symphony of music, the intellectual benefit he obtains from reading a book or going to college, the value he receives from a friendship, the spiritual hunger he satisfies in communing with God, are examples of this selfish love. Another type of love is unselfish; it does not want value from things and people, but rather desires to put value into unfortunate, needy persons and social situations. Jesus' parable of the lost coin illustrates what this unselfish, redemptive love is like: A lost coin has no value to itself or to anyone; but when the housewife seeks and finds the coin, she puts value into it. Christian love does that to individuals—it puts worth into them. Through his medical missionary work in Africa, Dr. Schweitzer is an incarnation of Christian love putting value into the needy, sick, unfortunate persons in that part of the world.

A Christian's world is as broad as his concern for mankind. The Christian sees the needs of the world as relative. In my student days at Marburg University in Germany in 1928–1929, I remember talking to German students about the relative conditions of wealth and poverty in the United States and Germany. In the United States we were living amidst superficial luxury; in Germany students wore patched clothes, ate meager meals, purchased only the necessities of life. The contrast was startling. Then one day I talked with a student from Poland; he told me how much better cared for were German students than those of Poland. In similar fashion, Pearl Buck said that she never believed poverty could be worse than in China, until her visit to India; there she observed more terrible hunger and pestilence. To those in need in our own neighborhoods, to those who live on other continents, Albert Schweitzer's "reverence for life" should minister.

"Reverence for life" was incarnate in Jesus Christ. It radiates to us today. Schweitzer feels that it is synonymous with true Christianity, and in the heart of Africa he is trying to live it: "Because I am devoted to Christianity in deep affection, I am trying to serve it with loyalty and sincerity." How safe we would feel today if atomic energy could be used in the world by men with Schweitzer's feeling of "reverence for life."

Frank C. Laubach 1884-

THREE-FIFTHS of the human race can neither read nor write. In Asia and Africa nine out of ten are illiterate. Over one billion people are enslaved within their little worlds because they cannot communicate through the written word. Yet progress toward literacy has been made in the last twenty years, in which time 100,000,000 have become literate. If this progress continues for fifty years, almost one half of the illiterate will be able to read and write by 2000 A.D. One who has done much to aid literacy is Frank Laubach.

In 1915 Frank Laubach with his wife went to the Philippine Islands; there he founded churches on the island of Mindanao and established Union College in Manila. It is estimated that through his educational efforts he has been able to teach one half of the 90,000 people on the island of Mindanao to read and write. Through teaching these people to become literate, he feels that he has found "a wonderful way to bring people to Christ. If you sit down beside an illiterate as your equal, your heart overflowing with love for him, and with a prayer on your lips that you may help him to a new vision; if you never frown nor criticize, but look pleased and surprised, and praise him for his progress, a thousand silver threads wind about his heart and yours. . . . Teaching illiterates is a means of extending the gospel, moreover, because every Christian needs to read his Bible."*

Communication of individuals through the written word

* Frank Laubach, *The Silent Billions Speak* (Friendship Press, 1922).

is a great urge in the world; an even greater need is the communication of men with God. In realizing this latter necessity, Frank Laubach said, "As I analyze myself I find several things happening to me as a result of these two months of strenuous effort to keep God in mind every minute. This concentration upon God is *strenuous*, but everything else has ceased to be so. I think more clearly, I forget less frequently. Things which I did with a strain before, I now do easily and with no effort whatever. I worry about nothing, and lose no sleep. I walk on air a good part of the time. Even the mirror reveals a new light in my eyes and face. I no longer feel in a hurry about anything. Nothing can go wrong excepting one thing. That is that *God may slip from my mind* if I do not keep on my guard. If He is there, the universe is with me. My task is simple and clear."*

Frank Laubach feels that if we could enlist 500,000,000 people to pray as they work, we could have a new impetus in our civilization. He suggests that we say "flash prayers," little prayers of ten seconds or a minute long when we awaken in the morning, as we bathe, as we dress, as we walk down stairs, when we ask the blessing at the table, as we leave the house, as we walk or ride to work, as we are on the elevator, between interviews, as we prepare for lunch, before we fall to sleep. Such times are events when we can "practice the presence of God." William L. Stidger wrote an article a few years ago entitled "Rest Where You Are," in which he pointed out that one of the cures for our tensions is the art of relaxation—we can relax when our car stops before the red light at a crossing, we can relax as we await an interview. This article was sent to the armed services throughout the world during World War II. In these

* Frank Laubach, *Letters to a Mystic*.

moments when we relax, work with our hands, make "flash prayers," we can direct our thoughts to God.

A popular article called "Prayer Is Power," written by Alexis Carrel, says that "prayer is the most powerful energy that one can generate. . . . Its results can be measured in terms of increased physical buoyancy, greater intellectual vigor, moral stamina. . . . Today, as never before, prayer is a binding necessity in the lives of men and nations. . . . If the power of prayer is again released and used in the lives of common men and women; if the spirit declares its aims clearly and boldly, there is yet hope that our prayers for a better world will be answered." Such a view is in accord with Frank Laubach's desire to mobilize half a billion people in prayer for a better world.

The Bible is translated into 1,055 languages for 95 per cent of the world. But only 40 per cent of the world's population can read and write. Only 15 per cent of the non-Christians are literate. Frank Laubach throws out a challenge to us in America to bring literacy to the world as an avenue of bringing God into the lives of these people. "America," he says, "you have the chance of ten thousand years to help the world! Our peace and world peace demand that we shall grow large enough and become Christlike soon enough to lavish our love in humble service for the whole world."

E. Stanley Jones 1884-

In september, 1942, I went to California for a series of lectures. Before boarding the train in Chicago I procured, among other books, *Abundant Living* by E. Stanley Jones. It was a book of daily devotional readings which attempted to help the individual "get along with himself." I found that the reading of this book during occasional moments each day enhanced the enjoyment and the restfulness of the journey. This excellent book of devotions met such a popular need that it sold 600,000 copies the first six years of its publication. I was so enthusiastic about the book that I gave a copy during World War II to each of my students when he entered the armed services. The book shows how with the Christian religion we can overcome our selfishness, fears, resentments, wrong desires, low motives, and find "abundant living."

E. Stanley Jones was born in Baltimore, Maryland, and educated at Asbury College, Kentucky. In 1907 he went to India and became a missionary of the high castes. In 1928 he was elected bishop of the Methodist Church, but declined the office in order to continue his missionary work. For many years he has conducted "ashrams" (religious retreats for small groups), where he has brought people of various religious faiths together for the purpose of discussing their experiences of God. In his evangelistic work, especially in North and South America, he has probably spoken to more people about Christianity than any other living person.

After Dr. Jones was a missionary in India for eight years,

he became ill, due to nervous exhaustion. He went to America on a year's furlough to recuperate. Upon returning to India after the furlough, he found himself unable to carry on his work. Listen to his story: "It was one of my darkest hours, at that time I was in a meeting at Lucknow. While in prayer, not particularly thinking about myself, a Voice seemed to say: 'Are you ready for this work to which I have called you?' I replied: 'No, Lord, I am done for. I have reached the end of my rope.' The Voice replied: 'If you will turn that over to me and not worry about it, I will take care of it.' I quickly answered: 'Lord, I close the bargain right here.' A great peace settled into my heart and pervaded me. I knew it was done! Life—abundant Life—had taken possession of me. I was so lifted up that I scarcely touched the road as I quietly walked home that night. Every inch was holy ground. For days after that I hardly knew I had a body. I went through the days, working all day and far into the night, and came down to bedtime wondering why in the world I should ever go to bed at all, for there was not the slightest trace of tiredness of any kind. I seemed possessed by Life and Peace and Rest—by Christ himself."* The test of E. Stanley Jones' conversion is shown in what his life became after this dramatic event. Certainly he had the right to write on the theme "abundant living."

Dr. Jones suggests nine steps by which a person climbs the ladder of prayer up to God:

1. Decide what you want from prayer

2. Ask yourself if this object you desire is a Christian object

* E. Stanley Jones, *The Christ of the Indian Road.* Copyright 1925 by Abingdon Press.

3. Write down what you want from prayer
4. Put your mind into a quiet, receptive mood
5. Talk with God about your need
6. Promise God how you will work with Him to make the prayer come true
7. Do everything loving which comes to your mind about it
8. Thank God for answering the prayer in His way
9. Release the prayer from the center of your thoughts, committing it to His care.

"Prayer," says E. Stanley Jones, "is not so much an act as an attitude. Prayer is opening the channels from our emptiness to God's fullness, from our defeat to his victory. The man who prays overcomes everything, for he is overcome by the most redemptive fact of the universe, the will of God."

At the heart of "abundant living" he suggests that we "let go, and let God," that we shift from self-centeredness to God-centeredness. Prayer is primarily a surrender to God, a trust in Him during all the events of life. Several years ago Dr. Jones was in an airplane, destined to land at Saint Louis. Due to bad weather conditions, the plane could not land. As the plane circled over the airport, with the gasoline tank nearing the empty mark, the passengers were told that there might be a crash landing. During this experience, Dr. Jones tells about his calmness. On a piece of paper he wrote his last testament to the effect that he was unafraid of what might happen; that as he had always trusted

God, he was trusting him in this moment of imminent danger. Fortunately the plane landed safely. But out of this experience an x ray was obtained of the soul of E. Stanley Jones who knew how to "let go and let God." It was a test that his conversion in Lucknow thirty-five years ago was lasting.

Toyohiko Kagawa 1888-1960

ABOUT TWENTY YEARS ago Toyohiko Kagawa spoke in the chapel at Princeton University. After the address a student was walking from the chapel with an older friend. Both were quiet for a short time; then the student remarked: "I had heard so much about Kagawa. After hearing him today, I am a bit disappointed. He didn't seem to say much." A moment later the student continued: "I noticed as he read the New Testament, that he held the pages close to his eyes." The older friend then asked: "Do you know why he held the page near his eyes? Some years ago, when Kagawa was living in the slums of Kobe, a beggar from the street asked Kagawa to give him shelter for the night. Kagawa let him stay that night in his shack, and caught a disease of the eyes, trachoma, from the vagrant; this disease almost blinded him. That is why he holds the printed word so close to his eyes." After a few quiet moments, the student replied: "Well, I guess a man doesn't need to say a great deal when he's hanging on a cross."

Among contemporary Christians who practice redemptive love in the unfortunate areas of society, Kagawa stands among the foremost. Born in Japan, he was educated in Japan and at Princeton Theological Seminary. From 1908 to 1923 he lived in the slums of Kobe, helping the downtrodden. Kagawa's work in the Kobe slums, his labor for cooperative societies in Japan, his role as a world evangelist, his loyalty to Christian ideals amid a Shinto civilization, mark him as one of the great saints of modern times. Defective in sight and frail in body, yet understanding the power of the Christian gospel, he is worthy to write *Meditations on the Cross.*

Kagawa derives lessons from the Cross. It teaches us that suffering comes from God as a means by which groups bear one another's burdens, thus turning pain into joy. It helps us use sorrow for a purpose. "The teachings of Christianity make it possible to endure sorrow with a heart at peace." The Cross helps us meditate on death, so that instead of being saddened by death, we are able to look into eternity. The Cross aids us to conquer selfishness and sin. "Christ's Cross is a Cross of victory. It is a Cross which causes man in death to be resurrected to God. The Cross is a crystallization of the love of God. If a character such as Christ's appears, man's failures can be forgiven. Looking at the Cross we can discern the great love of God to man."

A friend said of Kagawa, "He is a Christian idealist. He keeps his eyes on the stars. But he keeps his feet on the ground."* When war with Japan ceased in 1945, Kagawa (then fifty-seven) began a new life. The Christian Service Centers, which he had built in Kobe, Tokyo and Osaka, had been burned and bombed during the war. Military rule had abolished the labor unions he had organized. His program of reconstruction in the rural areas was spoiled. His peace movement had been abandoned. But once again today we find Kagawa, little in stature but great in spirit, as a special adviser to the Department of Public Welfare, and active in rebuilding the National Anti-War League. He refused to become a member of Premier Higashi-Kuni's cabinet or to run for Parliament, that he might remain a Christian preacher. "I must preach," he affirmed. "My father was a politician. As a youth I promised God that I would preach.

* William Axling, *Kagawa.* Copyright 1932, 1946 by Harper & Brothers.

I listen only to the inner voice." He feels that the way of Christ is the only solution for Japan and the world. "Humility and self-examination have returned to Japan. Japan must repent." Out of repentance in the heart of all men we can build a world Christian brotherhood.

Kagawa is a man of deep devotional living. Before World War II, when he was in the United States speaking and holding conferences for long hours each day, he would arise at four in the morning to spend several hours in meditation and spiritual reading. He is, however, no saint who wants to live in a monastery. He wants to "practice the presence of God" in the slums and in the marketplaces where social life throbs with problems. "Mountain retreats and religious systems can never constitute a Gospel. True salvation begins with the heart. If salvation is not realized in the crowd and in the bustling city, a true, living religion has not yet begun its work."

Born out of wedlock, an orphan at four, his body weakened by tuberculosis, partially blinded by trachoma, under five feet in height, half the weight of a college fullback, Toyohiko Kagawa is one of the spiritual giants of the modern world. He is a symbol of what Christians ought to be if the Kingdom of God is to come into the world.